GREAT ISSUES

CONCERNING FREEDOM

Edited and with an Introduction

By

WALDEMER P. READ

UNIVERSITY OF UTAH PRESS

Table of Contents

Foreword v

Introduction vii

What Are the Conditions of Freedom?   **1**   DANIEL J. DYKSTRA   1
   Comments:
      RICHARD G. HENSON 9
      FRANCIS D. WORMUTH 12

Need Our Sustained Posture of Defense
Jeopardize Our Freedoms?   **2**   JACK H. ADAMSON   15
   Comments:
      RICHARD B. KREUTZER 33
      OBERT C. TANNER 37

Is Freedom of the Press Compatible
With National Security?   **3**   NEAL A. MAXWELL   41
   Comments:
      HAYS GOREY 54
      WILLIAM B. SMART 57

What Are the Relations Between Freedom
and the National Economy?   **4**   JEWELL J. RASMUSSEN   61
   Comments:
      HENRY R. PEARSON 79
      ROBERT E. SMITH 85

Can We Educate for Freedom?   **5**   ASAHEL D. WOODRUFF   89
   Comments:
      ESTHER R. LANDA 104
      CHARLES H. MONSON, JR. 108

What Freedom Is Found in the Local Culture?   **6**   WALDEMER P. READ   113
   Comments:
      DAVID W. BENNETT 129
      THOMAS F. O'DEA 132
      LEWIS M. ROGERS 134

Foreword

The Great Issues Forum of the University of Utah was conceived and its program launched in response to a conviction in the minds of the members of the staff of the Department of Philosophy that university professors, though in some degree specialists, should have something important to say to the laymen of the community regarding questions of general interest and of vital current concern to the public.

The Forum is jointly sponsored by the Extension Division and the Department of Philosophy of the University of Utah and each year presents papers bearing upon facets of a central theme chosen for the year. The papers included in the volume here presented comprised the program for the Forum's ninth annual series (1961–1962). The theme was "Great Issues Concerning Freedom."

Though the form for an evening's program has varied from year to year and even within a given year, for 1961–62 the plan was to have the presentation of a main paper followed by remarks from two or more formally designated discussants or commentators, these presentations, in turn, to be followed by open discussions featuring audience participation. As will appear to even the casual observer, the remarks offered by the formal discussants turned out more often than not, though not always, to be supplementary in nature rather than specific criticisms or assessments of the main papers.

Of course it is not supposed that the general theme for the year is in any way exhausted by the papers presented. The number of facets of the theme to be treated was determined by programming considerations. The selection of specific items for treatment reflects judgments of importance, together with considerations of the interests and competences of persons available for inclusion on the program.

Those participating on the program, listed in the order of their appearance, were:

DANIEL J. DYKSTRA, *professor of law and academic vice-president of the university*

RICHARD G. HENSON, *assistant professor of philosophy*

FRANCIS D. WORMUTH, *professor and acting head of the department of political science*

JACK H. ADAMSON, *professor of English and dean of the College of Letters and Science*

RICHARD B. KREUTZER, *professor and head of the department of military science*

OBERT C. TANNER, *professor of philosophy*

v

NEAL A. MAXWELL, *instructor in political science and assistant to the president of the university*

HAYS GOREY, *news editor of the* Salt Lake Tribune

WILLIAM B. SMART, *editor of the editorial page of the* Deseret News *and* Telegram

JEWELL J. RASMUSSEN, *professor and head of the department of economics*

HENRY R. PEARSON, *executive director of the Utah Foundation*

ROBERT E. SMITH, *assistant professor of economics*

ASAHEL D. WOODRUFF, *professor of educational psychology and dean of the College of Education*

MRS. ESTHER R. LANDA, *member of the Board of Education, Salt Lake City Public Schools*

CHARLES H. MONSON, JR., *associate professor of philosophy*

WALDEMER P. READ, *professor and head of the department of philosophy*

DAVID W. BENNETT, *assistant professor of philosophy*

THOMAS F. O'DEA, *professor of sociology*

LEWIS M. ROGERS, *assistant professor of philosophy*

Introduction

For too long, perhaps, the abstract idea of freedom has been a subject of metaphysical debate. As considered in the discussions reported in this volume, however, freedom is a generalized ideal for human living. As such an ideal it is at once a product and an expression of the millenia-long history of rising human aspirations.

As a generalized ideal, freedom is an abstraction. It is not true that all men, or even most men, want it — not many want it very hard. What is wanted are the specific freedoms. For freedoms are many and diverse. Some are wanted by some men, and some by others. In any given case the freedom wanted is but the reverse side of a restraint, frustration or limitation felt. In such a case the freedom wanted is concrete; and it is often wanted *very* hard.

Men are free when the conditions and quality of their lives are of their own choosing. Genetically conceived, the idea of freedom is an intellectual formulation of the desire that the wish could be father to the fact. That is, man shares with other members of the animal kingdom a plight in which things are less than completely satisfactory. However, only man knows his plight; and even he, especially at first, knows it only sleepily and fitfully. Generally, an animal when caught can only thrash and fret; man, in contrast, can judge his predicament and scheme, successfully or not, for escape. Thus men have been in bondage, doing the bidding of others; and they have breathed to themselves, "If only we didn't have to." Men have been restricted; and their whispered response has been, "If only we could." They have been in want, and dreamed, "What if these stones were bread?" Or, in great pain and suffering, they have cried out, "Why does this have to be?" In varying degrees, and progressively, men have come to envisage a world more nearly to their liking. Progressively, men have dared to hope. In these ways they have differed from other animals. In his yen for freedom man manifests a power of transcendence not shared, not equally at least, by his animal brothers.

Of the many facets of this long, upward struggle with its slowly awakening aspirations and its even slower achievements — for, always, accomplishment lags behind envisagement — three, in particular should be noted: 1) endeavor to escape from domination by men, 2) rebellion against the limitations of nature, and finally, 3) man's search for freedom within himself.

1) At the beginning perhaps, and certainly through "aeons of forgotten time" thereafter, the domination of men by other men was taken for granted. Many and various have been the forms of subordination,

subjection, and exploitation to which men have been accustomed. But although as a general rule men habituated in subjection have taken subjection for granted; even so, it was often not without hatred; thus there has been a countertendency. Against established dominations and the hardships, inconveniences, and suffering which they entailed, individual men have reacted with resentment, and sometimes with scheming for escape. At first and usually, no doubt, such reactions were not based on principle; and they were not against institutions and practices as such; rather, they were personal. They were not so much rational as emotional. The run-away slave was not trying to destroy the institution of slavery so much as to better his own condition. The incident of the freed-man, no matter whether his freedom had been purchased or had been otherwise obtained, implied no accusation against the institution from which he had been freed. In general, no doubt, the condition prevailed which Plato would have described as fulfilling the requirements of temperance: there was agreement on the part of all as to who should rule.

But in the long run, through a long and tedious sequence of human events consisting of myriad acts, acts of brutality, escape, protest, insurrection, concession, compromise, granting of a charter, court order, etc.; a sequence of events in the course of which religions arose and underwent change and philosophies were propounded, criticized, and improved upon; a sequence marked by the emergence of a sense of history, and of a social consciousness and conscience, a transformation has occurred which is most remarkable for human life; namely, desire has been transmuted into principle, and personal discontent has given rise to rational disapproval.

But the rational man is an obligated man, since to act in deference to general principles is to subordinate the particular desires of the concrete, particular situation. Consequently, it can readily be understood why it is that the general ideal of freedom should find itself so often in conflict with the specific freedoms coveted by men — why it is that men so often oppose freedom in the interest of freedom. It seems simple to say that one man's freedom ends at the point where another man's freedom begins; but difficulty comes in working it out. Logically this saying seems to imply that in order to be universal, freedom must be limited. Government and freedom seem antithetical. To many, notably Plato, the idea of self-government has seemed paradoxical — the paradox being resolved only upon the assumption that the idea refers to "a whole" wherein the better elements rule and the less worthy are *subject to rule*. Government has meant dictatorship. In order that some might be free, others must be unfree. From this it is an easy step, to go with Marx, to the idea that the dictatorship of the bourgeoisie and the dictatorship of the proletariat are the only alternatives.

Under Plato's aristocratic interpretation of just government it was the state that was free, not the people. For a democratic resolution of the paradox of self-government we have Rousseau to thank. He showed how each and every individual can be at once sovereign and subject, ruler and ruled, free and governed, on the basis of the general will. Government and freedom are not antithetical when each man governs himself in the interest of the general good. No government is necessary beyond that which rational men will impose upon themselves. Lincoln's happy phrase "government of the people, by the people, for the people" makes good sense. Such government is possible when the people are united through an identity of interest and purpose. Such government is but the formal structure whose actions express the general will; and each man can be governed by it without being any the less free.

But the general will is an ideal. In fact men are not united by identity of interest and purpose except in the most general terms. Rather, diversity and conflict of interest characterize the social scene, locally, nationally, and internationally. In the experience of many, government is opposed to freedom.

Nevertheless a government of free men is theoretically possible. Indeed, it is already realized in some degree. For, even though only in general terms, still, in general terms men *are* united by identity of interest. What is lacking, needed, if we are to move nearer to the ideal? Several things. First, a more lively awareness, on the part of men generally, of such identity of interests as does exist — such awareness would transform these interests into consciously shared goals. Secondly, it is needed that individual men generally undergo a change of character such as will fit them for citizenship in a free society. This means that men must come to have increased ability and readiness to think and will in terms of the general good — the concept of the "socialized conscience." Thirdly, it means that institutions, practices and modes of operation, economic, political, etc., must be continuously and progressively altered so as to make them consistent with the general good. In the fourth place, it requires that the above transformations be effected through continued, and even increased functioning of "democratic dialogue," free and effective communication, and free participation by all who wish in the decision-making processes. Finally, it is requisite that there be increasing recognition that an essential feature of the general good is an atmosphere of opinion and practice that allows for and even encourages individuality, the development and pursuit of idiosyncrasy in tastes, practices, beliefs, and expressions. These last two mentioned considerations, particularly, are important to insure that in its practical working out the general will will take on a democratic and free character, rather than one that is authoritarian and totalitarian. This is where Rousseau failed.

2) Early man was overwhelmed by nature. Continuous with her in his being, he developed a sense, along with his emerging self-consciousness, of dependence upon her. Sunshine and rain, plant and animal growth, the changing seasons, earthquakes and volcanos, tornados and floods, plagues, pestilences, famines, and even wars — these all entered so vitally, decisively, authoritatively, into his experience that man's first mode of reaction was one of acquiescence. Though ignorant of causal law in the scientific sense early man developed concepts consistent with his experience of dependence. Such a concept was the Greek notion of fate. This idea was taken up, refined and elaborated in Stoicism into the concept of nature as a rational whole, the events and particulars of which were necessitated by the whole. Men learned to regard themselves as such necessitated items, and the events in their lives as beyond their control. Man's only freedom, it was understood, consisted in the rational acceptance of his plight. Nature, so conceived, easily took on connotations of divinity. Indeed, a religious analogue of the Stoic conception is reflected in the words of Job: ". . ., the Lord gave, and the Lord has taken away; blessed be the name of the Lord."

This is all changing significantly, with the development of modern science. Men are becoming increasingly confident that, within limits, they can manipulate nature and so order the conditions of life as to markedly alter the duration, quality, and value of individual human lives. Nay, not only are men confident that this can be done, but their confidence is confirmed by the fact that it has already been done to a considerable degree. On the average, particularly in the western world, human life today is longer, safer, healthier, less characterized by suffering, more enjoyable, more varied, more filled with opportunity for choice than ever before. Nature still pushes him around; but man need no longer resign himself to a fate that is altogether beyond his altering. With the recognition that, in the words of Francis Bacon, "knowledge is power" and that we can "command nature" if we will only learn to "obey her," man has increased his freedom immensely, and may increase it even more — within limits perhaps, but within limits unknown —

limits that serve chiefly to argue for a certain kind of humility toward nature, a recognition that we must respect her and learn to obey her, which, translated, means recognition of the importance of cultivating the scientific attitude and a knowledge and habituation in the use of scientific method.

3) Freedom, in its more important meaning, is not a mere matter of man's relation to persons and things external to himself. Rather, it is an attribute of character. That a man should be free in himself, this is the first great moral concern. To have positive power of rational choice and effective performance; to be a "fully functioning" individual able to face the world rationally and see the situations of life, not through the spectacles of psychotic or neurotic distortion, but adequately as they are in fact; this is the ideal condition, a condition upon which ability to act effectively in the interest of other freedoms is dependent.

The notion that men are often victims of inner bondage, together with the correlative ideal of freedom within, is not new in history. In ancient times the lack of inner freedom was often thought to be the work of evil spirits. It was understood that a devil or devils may take possession of a man. Of course the dominant Christian conception is that expressed in the words of Jesus, "Whosoever committeth sin is the servant of sin." Or, in the words of St. Paul, "So then it is no longer I that do it, but sin that dwelleth in me." But what is new in this connection is that which is represented by the nascent science of psychiatry; namely, the substitution of the concept of illness for sin, together with the assumption that mental illnesses have specific causes which are susceptible to analysis and understanding.

Finally, though moral freedom is an attribute of character, it is not unrelated to the culture in which the individual develops. For if illnesses have their causes, so also does health depend upon conditions which are conducive to it. Psychiatry and related studies are already pointing beyond therapy to the need of a sociology of mental health — and, it would seem reasonable to suppose, to an economics of mental health. As we become aware that malfunctioning individuals are symptomatic of social and economic conditions that are less than optimum for character development, this conception will become an important consideration in the statesman's conception of the general good. Children reared in destitute circumstances have at least two strikes against them. But if indigence is unfavorable to the development of moral freedom, so also is opulence in the presence of indigence.

1

What Are the Conditions of Freedom?

DANIEL J. DYKSTRA

The late Learned Hand, writing in 1930, observed that man "is tied to all men, as all men are tied to him, in a web whose threads no eye can follow and no fingers can unravel." Time has accentuated the validity of this comment, and in its validity rests the complications and ramifications of the topic with which the Great Issues Forum will be concerned during the next few months.

The day is far past when we can conceive of an individual molding his fate independent of his fellow man. His acts occur in a context of relationships, and thus, of necessity, they cast a shadow on many, and in turn what many do casts a shadow on him. It is understandable, therefore, that individuals are sensitive, in varying degrees, to the attitudes and actions of others, for in such attitudes and actions rests their own well-being.

These observations have even greater validity in the area of international relations. While we have traditionally underestimated our degree of involvement in world affairs, events since World War II have served to alert all who have respect for facts to the realization that the destiny of the United States is inextricably tied to the ebb and flow of world events. Laos, South Vietnam, Berlin, Formosa, Egypt, Cuba, Korea, Syria, and the Congo are names which ring as harsh, discordant reminders that waves of cause and effect stemming from incidents throughout the globe reach our shores with undiminished force. We may dream nostalgically of a simpler day, but such dreams are quickly dissipated by the grim presence of reality.

This interdependency of people and nations naturally has an impact in terms of freedom — in terms, that is, of the right of each to think, to speak, and to act independently of others. Unfortunately, this interaction in modern society cannot be ignored, and even those of us who plead for broad latitude of individual choice recognize that because of it limitations do and must exist. Our difference with those who would be more restrictive is therefore a variance in degree, but *that degree* is a matter of fundamental significance.

It would, of course, be unrealistic to assume that citizens of this country could experience the events and developments of the past thirty

1

years without reassessing the proper role of the individual to his government and to other members in society. We have witnessed this reassessment in many congressional investigations concerned with internal security, in a series of legislative enactments, state and national, aimed at various associations and activities, and in a host of court decisions relating to individual rights. More recently we have witnessed this reassessment by many private groups who are actively engaged in making pronouncements on what is "American" and what is "Un-American," what is "patriotic" and what is "not patriotic."

Before commenting on the significance of these activities, it is appropriate to include a brief reminder of the premise on which our government was founded. That premise is simply that a society functions best when its members have a maximum degree of freedom to speak, to write, and to associate as their judgment dictates. A profound belief in this concept prompted the adoption of the first eight amendments to the Constitution. The first amendment spells out in explicit terms five areas in which individuals are to be free from congressional prohibitions. That amendment states: "Congress shall make no law respecting an establishment of religion, or prohibiting the free exercise thereof; nor shall Congress make any law which abridges freedom of speech, or the press, or the right of the people peaceably to assemble, or the right to petition the government for a redress of grievances." This profound respect for the individual is further reflected in subsequent amendments which prohibit unreasonable searches, which assert that no person in a criminal case shall be compelled to be a witness against himself, which guarantee due process of law, and which unequivocably state that an accused has the right to be confronted by his accusers.

In making these pronouncements, the framers of the Constitution were seeking to perpetuate a philosophy which centered not on the authority of government but rather on the rights of each member of society. They were, in Justice Jackson's words, hoping to withdraw certain rights "from the vicissitudes of political controversy, to place them beyond the reach of majorities and officials and to establish them as legal principles to be applied by the courts."

The justice's words suggest a further observation concerning the purpose which motivated the adoption of the Bill of Rights. These amendments were not designed as a charter to protect the rights of majorities, for majorities are usually capable of self-protection. They were designed to encompass the unorthodox, the nonconformist, the lonely person whose views are fighting to be heard. They were, to use the words of the great Justice Storey, adopted as an "important protection against unjust and oppressive conduct on the part of the people themselves."

From what has been said, it is obvious that the motivating force which prompted those who founded our government was the assumption that a maximum degree of individual freedom was the best guarantee of an enlightened society. It is also apparent that they assumed that such freedom would give strength and sustaining power to a newly formed government. That freedom entailed risks, they well knew, but these risks they were willing to accept, for they also knew from personal experience that the dangers inherent in authoritarian government were far greater. Furthermore their respect for man's dignity, for his mental and spiritual well-being, for his peace of mind, for the unfolding of his personality gave them no real alternative to the choice which they made.

The passage of time has lent validity to their judgment. While many governments have come and gone, ours has continued through wars, depressions, and other crises for over a hundred and seventy years. For the most part, we have, during this period, remained faithful to our heritage. There have, however, been exceptions. One need but recall the Alien and Sedition Acts of John Adams' administration, the suppression of habeas corpus proceedings during the Civil War, the restrictions on liberty during World War I, and the Palmer raids of the early 1920's to recognize that on occasion we have resorted to actions not wholly compatible with our pronouncements on individual liberty. Whether any such actions were necessary is a matter for conjecture. The fact is we did indulge in them, and we did so in the belief that by so doing we were enhancing our security.

It is in this observation that I find greatest concern for the status of freedom in our time. Heretofore, most actions which were restrictive of liberty were associated with emergencies which were of a transient nature. There was thus reason to hope that their passing would produce a restoration of individual rights. Fortunately, such hopes were well founded, for, with few exceptions, our society hastened to reassert its established beliefs after each crisis had run its course.

It would be reassuring to state that this pattern will continue, that any concessions made today in the name of security will be a temporary adjustment. A realistic appraisal does not warrant such optimism. It must be recognized that the world of the present is not the world of fifty, of twenty-five, or even of ten years ago. Increased interdependence coupled with the development of grim and fantastic weapons capable of mass destruction make it folly to assume that current emergencies are of a temporary nature. Many nations have the capacity to build crisis on crisis, and the evidence of the past few years suggests that certain of these countries are not reluctant to utilize such power. We cannot, therefore, sacrifice certain freedoms on the easy assumption that within a short time they will be restored, for if anything seems predictable, it is that we face many years of uncertainty and conflict.

The question which thus confronts us is whether in an age such as this we can adhere to the basic faith upon which our nation was founded, that faith which rests its confidence in the individual and his freedom. This is, I believe, today's crucial issue. What is more, it is being resolved by the struggle currently in existence between those who would narrow the areas of personal liberty and those who seek to prevent such constriction. It is this tug-of-war which is shaping the blueprint for tomorrow's society.

In appraising this struggle, we must recognize that it is not to be characterized by sudden and dramatic episodes. Rather the danger to liberty lies in the gradual erosion of individual rights. As Justice Jackson observed, ". . . traditional freedoms are less in danger of any sudden overthrow than in being gradually bartered or traded for something else on which the people place a higher current value."

Because areas of freedom are thus restricted, there exists the very real possibility that the withering of rights may proceed for years before its impact is fully realized. In truth, it is my impression that many who today plead for restrictive action in the name of security do so without recognizing that they are contributing to the chipping away of rights, rights which heretofore have been our proudest boast. Justice Douglas was unfortunately correct when he observed: "History shows that the main architects of repressive laws were often men of good intentions."

A closer look at the contemporary scene may emphasize some of the observations already made. It may also serve to illustrate that the current conflict concerning freedom is more than an academic discussion, that even as it proceeds repercussions result which have a direct impact on our nation's welfare.

Those concerned with present developments are aware that today's resurgent voices, of those who view with suspicion and alarm concepts which they have labeled as unacceptable, are to be contrasted with the voices that asserted themselves a decade ago. The drive for conformity in the early 1950's was sparked primarily by a few individuals and by congressional investigations. Present activities, however, are characterized by numerous private organizations representing many people operating in a variety of ways. This means that the forces of restriction are broader based, are more diffuse, and are more deeply entrenched than was formerly the case.

Before making further comment, I should like it clearly understood that I am not questioning the right of any person or any private organization to espouse the views to which I make reference. Furthermore, I am of the impression that most of these voices are motivated by a genuine concern for our welfare and for our security. I do, however, believe that their endeavors are fraught with dangers, that in balance they are self-defeating and productive of harmful consequences.

These consequences are admittedly intangible and difficult to assess. This does not mean that they are insignificant. On the contrary, the fact that they must be measured in terms of suppressed ideas, in terms of fear and suspicion, in terms of unspoken criticism, and in terms of support withdrawn from worthy objectives such as the promotion of civil rights is in itself evidence of their gravity.

One does not have to search far to find specific examples. It is my impression that the reason we hear such limited discussion of this country's policies in respect to Communist China is the fact that proponents of any modification fear that the voicing of their views will result in accusations of disloyalty. For comparable reasons, it is difficult to find objective and unemotional assessments of our relationship to the Soviet Union, and it is equally difficult to hear constructive appraisals of the work of the House Un-American Activities Committee. When we recall that the premise on which our society operates is that solutions are best found in free and unintimidated exchange of views, it is apparent that great dangers lurk in the limited discussion of these and other significant topics.

A further reason why the current build-up of suspicion and intimidation should be of much concern is that it is producing two seemingly antithetical results. One product is rash, ill-timed action; the other is a paralysis of action. In reference to the first product, I point out that at the very time we should be exercising restraint and carefully exploring new ideas, policy makers and organs of public opinion are being prodded into extreme pronouncements and rash decisions. Do I over-dramatize? I submit the Cuban fiasco as a prime illustration.

Equally dangerous, however, is the possibility that loose charges of subversion and disloyalty are and will produce inaction. It is understandable, for example, that many members of our State Department are reluctant to voice new proposals or to modify existing policies. To do so may simply result in further harassment. The result is that instead of flexibility, there is rigidity; instead of new ideas, old solutions are repeated *ad nauseam*.

The above comment is not to suggest that the State Department is beyond criticism. Far from it. Its policies should be carefully analyzed and subjected to extensive discussion. My plea is simply that we refrain from wild, irresponsible accusations unrelated to the merits of any given policy. Such criticism serves no constructive purpose and can only lead to unfortunate results.

Another consequence stemming from the clamor currently being voiced by both extremes of the political spectrum is that it is making people reluctant to engage in the promotion of significant activities. The "guilt by association" advocates have convinced many individuals that organizations are to be judged not by their goals but rather by the political views of every member. Thus many are reluctant to engage in the battle for racial nondiscrimination for fear that in doing so they may find themselves in the company of one who has been labeled a radical. Others are equally reluctant to join battle with the forces urging vigilance in respect to other individual rights, and I fear from recent comment that the day may not be too remote, in fact it may already be here, when this same reticence will exist in respect to groups organized to support the United Nations and its objectives.

Please do not assume from these observations that I am unaware of the fact that Communists and other nefarious political forces have on occasion infiltrated and manipulated groups ostensibly dedicated to Civil Rights, nondiscrimination and other worthy goals. Obviously this has been and is being done. To conclude, however, that all organizations devoted to these causes are suspect, and that therefore all their members are to be viewed with suspicion, is wholly unwarranted. Such suspicion, with the accompanying reluctance on the part of many to lend support to meritorious objectives, is too high a price to pay. In an age when the pursuit of worthy ends must have collective support in order that progress may be made, we cannot afford to hurl charges indiscriminately at groups or individuals committed to their attainment, nor can we realistically decline to support just causes because they happen to correspond with the announced objectives of the Communists.

An additional product of the current wave of unrest is its impact on academic freedom. While this is not unrelated to the limited public discussion of certain grave national and international issues to which reference has already been made, it is, nonetheless, sufficiently distinctive to warrant special comment. No educational institution can be true to itself without freedom of inquiry and freedom of discussion. If members of its faculty are afraid to explore the avenues of truth wherever they may lead and are discouraged from engaging in the analyses of controversial topics, it is self-evident that it cannot perform its proper role as a center for the exploration and dissemination of knowledge and for the development of critical thought. Its faculty under such circumstances must of necessity be frustrated and lose its vitality; its students, also of necessity, will be untrained for that independent appraisal of complex issues so essential to a vigorous society.

In considering this aspect of the contemporary scene, we must recognize that limitations placed on academic freedom in one area of inquiry will have an immediate impact in other areas. Ideas and subject matter cannot be carved into parts, one part labeled acceptable, the other part unacceptable. Concepts are inextricably related to other concepts, and thus prohibition of discussion and investigation in one sphere automatically means prohibition of discussion and inquiry in other spheres. It thus is evident that what appears initially as a limited restriction soon mushrooms into a broad prohibition. To recognize the validity of this observation it is only necessary to recall the many activities and views which were considered suspect before the wave of hysteria which swept this country in the eary 1950's began to subside.

It will of course be argued by those who currently express anxiety as to views which they consider unorthodox that they are not seeking to subvert academic freedom. This underestimates the impact of their activities. When liberal views are equated with communism, when conclusions are suspect because they do not square with preconceived ideas, when whole areas of discussion are considered unsafe, academic freedom is being restricted and the pursuit of knowledge is being hampered.

In expressing alarm at these developments, I want to stress that my concern is not confined to their impact on the academic community. Of greater importance is the fact that academic scholarship and opinion cannot be suppressed without affecting the national interest. This is especially true in a society which has come to rely upon educational institutions for research, for facts, for analysis, and for opinions. To curtail by intimidation or other means the sources from and through which these results emanate will inevitably restrict both the quality and the quantity of information available to society and its functioning agencies.

It is hoped that these comments will not be construed to imply that I consider the views of any faculty member beyond criticism. Quite the opposite. The whole foundation of academic freedom rests on vigorous, searching criticism of any concept which is advanced. To deny this is the antithesis of freedom of inquiry and discussion. My objection is simply directed at the individual and groups currently critical of academic endeavors who direct their shots not at the validity or invalidity of various proposals but rather at the persons advancing them. In too many instances, these critics, while ignoring the merits of ideas with which they are not in sympathy, answer with broad, loose personal charges which by their very nature arouse suspicion and fear. That this is occurring will, I beieve, be supported by most close observers of the academic scene.

A further device utilized by those whose actions promote apprehension and misunderstanding is that of gross oversimplification of history and of national and international issues. This is objectionable first of all because it violates the integrity of knowledge. To explain, for example, Cuba and China solely in terms of Communist-anti-Communist ideologies and activities without recognizing the complex social, economic, and political backgrounds out of which their present governments emerged only serves to promote and perpetuate historical distortion. More unfortunately such explanations obscure the truly significant lesson that is to be learned from these experiences, for they conceal and de-emphasize the conditions which give rise to authoritarian control. This observation is also valid in reference to those who seek to reduce all contemporary problems, no matter how complex, to a clash of conflicting philosophies. Oversimplified explanations lead to oversimplified solutions. In turn, these result in false hopes and prevent the exploration and discussion of realistic remedies.

Before concluding, let me comment on another observation all too frequently heard in this day of uncertainty. This observation, stated in a variety of ways, is simply that true "Americanism" consists of but a single path. This monistic concept automatically means that those who differ are tarred with the brush of suspicion. It aso means that there is little room for the nonconformist, the unorthodox, the reformer. Furthermore, it overlooks the basic fact that heretofore our strength has been in pluralism, in the fact that as a society we have encouraged diversity of opinion in the belief that from such diversity we can distill those concepts which have the greatest merit.

Harold Taylor, former president of Sarah Lawrence College, has expressed this point of view in the following words:

Our greatest strength as a country lies in the fact that we have a diversity of opinion and diversity of people. We can absorb and use ideas of all kinds provided we keep ourselves in a situation in which every idea can have public expression. What has given this country's thought its vitality in the past is the continued struggle of men and women to gain acceptance for their own views, and the continual push of a variety of minority opinions. What marks our history from that of other countries is the way in which we have been able to avoid an orthodoxy, to remain open-minded and flexible, to absorb radical ideas in the flow of social process and to put them to work when they are needed.

In concluding, I want to stress that what has been said should in no way imply that I am unaware of the perils which confront us. Quite the opposite is true. It is because of such awareness that I urge, as I do, respect for our traditional freedom and for the dignity of the individual. To sacrifice such respect in this critical period will weaken our confidence in one another, will promote hostility between groups and between individuals, will distort our vision and lessen our resolve, will, in truth, make us less able to cope with the crisis of our times.

What I am saying is simply that our strength is in our freedom. Allen Barth, in his book *The Loyalty of Free Men* recognized this fact in the following words:

Individual freedom is . . . a means, an invaluable means, towards national security and survival. . . . It is an end as well — a supreme end which the government of the United States was instituted to secure. Faith in freedom as a means and as an end must be the ultimate touchstone of American loyalty, of the loyalty of all free men.

Comments

RICHARD D. HENSON

I am always suspicious of talk about national character, especially where the nation is made up of as many racial and cultural and religious strains, economic interests, and so on, as this one is. But — with this apology — I will remark that we must beware of certain strains in the American character under such conditions as are before us.

Our great folk-hero, the western U.S. marshal or the sheriff, faced with the evil bullying of the bad guys, does not waste his time in parley with them, trying to reach accommodations and make arrangements to avoid bloodshed or to win, over a decade of tactful talk and modest deeds, the friendship of wavering elements of the town. He deals with no skein of conflicting rights and claims, no history of enmity which poisons the good works of today, no ideological divisions (except perhaps that between cattle-men and sheep-men) that make understanding tenuous. There are bad guys and good guys, and they all know which is which.

The bad guys may be big and technically competent, and they may even kill some good guys, but that is all. If they are bad enough, they must be ordered out of town; if they resist, war is imminent; if they draw, they must die.

It is entirely fitting that the monster three-hour telecast and broadcast of a few weeks ago, laying down policies for Americans to follow in their fight with communism, came out of Hollywood, the original home of this western sheriff. For even in the old West, I suppose, things were hardly ever this simple; and today things are not simple at all.

I am afraid that we are not, as a nation, well fitted for the protracted struggle that we are involved in, requiring, as it does, not only courage but patience in the face of harassment and uncertainty and partial defeat. I suggest that the frustration and fear which many Americans feel today, and which many betray by their yearning for simple solutions, even at the cost of violence — a violence such as surpasses anything we can imagine — may come in part from the infantile illusion that America, God's chosen land, is naturally and essentially omnipotent, that no mere foreigner could ever be clever and strong enough to get ahead of us without our connivance, and that God would never let it happen that anyone would get ahead of us through what we might call the "accidents of history." From this premise, one moves easily to two false and dangerous conclusions: the first is that whenever anything goes badly for us — whether it be a student demonstration in San Francisco, a race riot in Detroit, the development of a bomb in Russia, or a military defeat in Vietnam — it must be the result of treachery here at home. The second false and pernicious belief which seems to follow from this sense of our natural omnipotence is that we can afford to cut ourselves loose from these aggravating allies and neutrals who constantly impede us, and that if the bad guys won't give in, we can just biff them in the nose. Why should we worry about winning friends, when we are the good guys? Why should we worry about the bomb either?

I can express some sympathy with some aspects of these views. We must, of course, be on guard against treachery and subversion at home. No informed person can doubt that Communist spies and the native

Communist party are agents of subversion. I grant that our allies and neutrals are distressing indeed, at times — although I should in fairness add (*a*) that we no doubt distress them often too, and (*b*) that I have not myself known even any person, much less any club, party, or nation, who did not find his (or its) fellow beings distressing a good deal of the time. And, a a third concession, while I should be glad to be convinced that I am wrong, I do not see how we can avoid going ahead with our preparations for little wars and for the big war.

So much I can concede to those who seem to me to believe in the notion of our essential omnipotence. But, of course, we are not omnipotent: there is much in the world that we cannot control, no matter how wise and firm our actions. There is much that will happen to distress and frighten us that we will not be able to do much about. And among the things we *can* do, waving the flag and shouting that we hate sin will be among the least effectual.

What then can we do? My suggestions will be very vague and general. We can try to inform ourselves, as far as we are able, about the world in which we live. We can try to keep our nerve and reconcile ourselves to living in a trying time, knowing that our trial will not end soon, unless it ends in catastrophe. We can take whatever part our talents and training and strength permit, in the effort to strengthen our country and to bring it closer to our ideal of it. We can be alert and unafraid in speaking up against demagoguery and obscurantism and plain silliness.

Can we win? That invites the question, can we win what? Can we win our struggle with the Communist empire? It is a curious question: because our only hope of survival lies in a protracted struggle through so long a period of time that it is hard to imagine what may happen to the world before it is over; it is hard to say, at this distance, what will constitute winning and what will constitute losing. But we can be sure of a few things: if, in waging this battle, we lose our right of dissent, our right to something in the way of privacy and an inner life which permits variety of personality, and of religion, and of opinion, we will have lost what makes this civilization worth preserving. And if we do not now, on every suitable occasion, stand up against the demagoguery and obscurantism which threatens this country — if we will not risk and sacrifice what needs to be risked and sacrificed in this domestic struggle — we will not preserve what is worthwhile in this country, nor will we deserve to.

FRANCIS D. WORMUTH

There are many who believe that our main domestic struggle is one between those who attach primary value to liberty and those who practice suppression in the interest of security. They argue that the latter group is shortsighted, that security is best achieved through freedom, that national conduct is possible only when all available information, all possible analyses and points of view are presented to the public.

No educated person would deny that the dubious and precarious advances that the human race has made through history would have been impossible without innovators like Socrates and Jesus Christ and Bruno and Joseph Smith, who have defied received opinion and paid with their lives for their offence. But these innovators were in fact guilty of a genuine offence against security. They threatened the *psychological security* which is afforded by traditional belief and a traditional social order. Freedom is always incompatible with *this* security.

I suggest that the security which many Americans prefer to freedom today is not *national* security or *physical* security. For fourteen years we have been engaged in an arms race of unprecedented size and velocity, which cannot possibly end in anything but national and physical extinction. This extinction may well be at hand in the dispute over Berlin. During these fourteen years those who posit security as the highest value have advocated no alternative to this suicidal course; on the contrary, they have been the loudest advocates of world suicide.

What, then, is the security they seek? They seek to return to a world in which there is no Soviet Union, no United Nations, no income tax, no labor unions, no social security, no demand for racial equality, no fluoridation of the water supply; to return, that is, to the McKinley Administration. This is to be accomplished by the compulsory affirmation of group values. The security they seek is the *psychological security of the crowd*.

It is a mistake to suppose that all men or most men value freedom. Many men value constraint, not only for others but for themselves. The psychological work reported by Marie Jahoda and others in *The Authoritarian Personality* shows that there is a distinct and coherent personality type which seeks group prescription of opinion and desires a rigid hierarchical social order resting on constraint and inequality.

A beetle is negatively phototropic and positively thigmotropic — that is to say, it shuns the light and is comfortable only when it is pressed front and back by tree and bark or earth and stone. The authoritarian personality is negatively phototropic. Whereas John Milton saw an

England practicing free opinion as an "eagle mewing in her mighty youth" and purging and unscaling her eyes at the very fount of heavenly radiance, the authoritarian personality shuns the light of free opinion; it seeks an imposed creed. The authoritarian personality is also positively thigmotropic. It seeks the comforting pressure and the unyielding support of an authoritarian social order.

The book *The Authoritarian Personality* attributes the emergence of this character to childhood experience. But a disturbing environment which leaves the individual frightened, unoriented, and alone will cause many normal adults to seek what Erich Fromm has called an *Escape from Freedom*. Fromm equates the search for psychological security with fascism, and shows that it can sweep away whole nations. In these terms, the issue is not between freedom and security in any rational sense of the word security; it is between freedom and unfreedom, with the escape from freedom pursued as a goal desirable in itself.

Here is ground for deep pessimism. Advocacy of freedom cannot avail with people who fear freedom and seek unfreedom. When security is equated to the comforting psychological experience of unfreedom, it is pointless to show that freedom is the avenue to a rational security, for rational security is not what is desired.

2

Need Our Sustained Posture of Defense Endanger Our Freedoms?

JACK H. ADAMSON

From the beginning, the American was doomed to come to terms with "bigness." He was never to know the small, communal intimacies of a Swiss canton where borders and boundaries continually made precise and secure definitions of property, of government and of the possibilities of life itself. He came to a land that was too big to manage. Again and again he tried to limit the scope of his problem by declaring that the boundary of this nation ought to be the Allegheny Mountains, the Great American Desert (whatever that was supposed to be), or the Rocky Mountains; but as fast as he absorbed and came to terms with Ohio or Oregon, some adventurer wished to purchase Alaska, annex Louisiana or conquer Texas. The reasons for the latter, especially, continue to prove puzzling.

In the nineteenth century the industrial revolution begot a similar bigness in corporations and industry. The intricacies, needs and potentialities of big business helped bring on big government which, although a much newer phenomenon, begins to seem to many people to be a kind of leviathan of the deep, ready to devour everything else. Bigness in industry and bigness in government, both have called, and continue to call, for restrictions and limits, new rules and a new set of attitudes, for changes in laws and in our mode and practice of government.

But the newest "bigness" in American life is in the sphere of the military establishment. Here the problem is scarcely ten years old, and therefore it has not begun to engender the severe reactions which, in the past, have arisen to meet the shifts of power in business and government. But such reaction is bound to come; in my opinion it is already overdue. This altogether unprecedented new source and focus of power in the military establishment will overflow and fill up other areas of our national life unless, by legislation or by an effort of the national will, we consciously erect new barriers or revitalize older attitudes which will contain this new power structure in ways which accord with the history of our nation, the intent of its founders, and the spirit of its laws. And we must begin to do this now, for in recent times the military establish-

15

ment has begun to depart, in certain radical ways, from its traditional functions.

In his final message to the nation before leaving office, President Eisenhower said:

This conjunction of an immense military establishment and a large arms industry is new in the American experience. The total influence — economic, political, even spiritual — is felt in every city, every State house, every office of the Federal government. We recognize the imperative need for this development. Yet we must not fail to comprehend its grave implications.

In the councils of government, we must guard against the acquisition of unwarranted influence, whether sought or unsought, by the military-industrial complex. The potential for the disastrous rise of misplaced power exists and will persist.

We must never let the weight of this combination endanger our liberties or democratic processes. We should take nothing for granted. Only an alert and knowledgeable citizenry can compel the proper meshing of the huge industrial and military machinery of defense with our peaceful methods and goals, so that security and liberty may prosper together.

Before I discuss further the implications of this new power structure, I should like to place the role of the military into some kind of historical perspective. Our founding fathers inherited a mistrust of militarism that almost bordered on the pathological. Much of the Bill of Rights was a direct result of the American experience of a tyranny in their former homeland, an invasion of their civil liberties that would have been impossible if the King of England had not had a standing army to enforce his decrees and prevent resistance to his unlawful acts. Because of their historical memories, the legislators of the state of Pennsylvania stated in the Bill of Rights of their constitution "that standing armies are dangerous to liberty, and ought not to be kept up in time of peace." A similar declaration was embodied in the constitution of the state of North Carolina. The framers of the Constitution for the United States tended to be of a similar mind and they were inclined to try to provide for the common defense with a militia, with volunteers, and to reject the idea of a standing army. Further, they made it a part of the Bill of Rights that every colonist was entitled to have his own musket or squirrel rifle; that is, to bear arms in his own defense.

This tendency to reject a standing army disturbed the leading Federalist, Alexander Hamilton, and he argued in the Federalist case for a small but permanent army. He based his case on a single, persuasive, overriding reason. Whatever dangers such an army might bring, and Hamilton acknowledged that they were considerable, the dangers were even greater without it. I think that he was right then, and I think that what he said is still true today. We cannot, at the moment, in the face of the threat of force from the Communist bloc, abolish or even seriously diminish our military establishment. For the moment, and probably for the foreseeable future, we must live with it. But we must try to live with it as wisely and as warily as possible.

Hamilton knew well enough why the colonists rejected the idea of a Federal army. The colonists, he said, remembered how Charles II and James II had used a standing army to deprive their ancestors of their civil liberties. Hamilton's explanation is partly true, but as Robert Frost has said, "There is always something more." And the something more in this case was the historical events Hamilton alluded to and also a tradition and a vision.

The tradition and the vision concern the role of the English yeoman archer in the great battles of Poitiers, Crecy and Agincourt in the four-teenth and fifteenth centuries. In these battles, the massed chivalry of France, noblemen encased in armor and mounted on chargers, advanced with insolent and arrogant pride against relatively small numbers of English freemen, yeomen, archers, whose right arms could draw their bows of yew the full length of yard-long arrows. These yeomen loosed shaft after shaft, first at a distance in a silvery arc and then at closer range, with a deadly hissing accuracy that penetrated buckler and breast-plate, that overthrew horse and rider. Unarmored and with only im-provised fortifications, they won England's great battles by the strength of their arm and the keenness of their eye. And when they returned to England, they did not return as serfs. Men who had proved their manli-ness and courage on foreign fields were not to be enslaved at home. When the vision of the yeoman archer became embodied in the legends of Robin Hood, it became clear that this newly won independence was the most treasured thing in the life of the yeoman and that it made him the equal of the Sheriff of Nottingham or any of the nobles of the land. Although the legends were historically false, they did not falsify the vision of the people of England who came to rely not upon large mili-tary establishments but upon the freedman who owned and worked his own land and who wore across his shoulders a weapon which he could afford or even make himself and one which he had so brilliantly mastered.

This ancient dream continued to animate the American colonists; only here it was the yeoman farmer whom Jefferson counted on to keep alive the spirit of freedom. Here it was the freeman, not with the bow and arrow, but with the musket, the flintlock, and later the rifle, and no one was able to convince the American people or the Congress for over a hundred years that the free man bearing his own arms was not this nation's best defense. But the dream, alas, ultimately died; the vision faded into the common light of day. In fact the very tenacity with which we clung to this dream, as Hamilton once remarked and as I shall demonstrate, on more than one occasion very nearly cost us our freedom.

In addition to this dream, there were perhaps three historical events which, more than any others, haunted the minds of the American colonists. The first concerned Oliver Cromwell's New Model army. At the beginning of 1647, the English Civil War had been won by the Puritan party. The vanquished Royalist army, the army of King Charles I, was disbanded, but what of the victorious army? The Puritan Parliament proposed to disband it, but without adequate guarantees for long arrears of pay and with no plan for the absorption of the veterans into the civil life of the nation. Of course there was always Ireland and a bright parliamentarian proposed that the victorious veterans might go fight in that unhappy land under some different commanders. There the rate of attrition from plague, ague and Celtic kerns might be sufficiently high that the Puritan Parliament could cease to worry about the Puritan veterans. But the army had other ideas. Deeply resentful of the manifest ingratitude of the nation, the army began a kind of grass roots political movement that had enormous implications for the future. First, each regiment appointed two political representatives who were called "agitators" and these agitators were instructed to secure two things. First, of course, the back pay, and second, "liberty of conscience." As one writer of the time said, "Some of the soldiers do not stick to call the Parliament men tyrants." It was Cornet Joyce, in direct collusion with the military agitators, who seized the person of the King. In June, 1647, army units advanced and threatened the city of London, demanding as condition for their withdrawal that eleven Presbyterians should be expelled from Parliament. These eleven voluntarily withdrew in order to save the city. But this was only the beginning. Sensing that a majority in the duly elected Parliament was hostile to it, the army, under the leadership of Colonel Pride, conducted a purging of the Parliament known as "Pride's Purge." In this purge, over one hundred members of Parliament who were "favorable to the King," which meant that they were opposed to his execution, were expelled from Parliament, and that the King was ultimately executed. And so Englishmen learned something about a standing army which they and their colonial descendants never forgot: that no element of civil government, neither the Parliament elected under the majesty of law, nor the sacred person of the sovereign, could withstand the threat of force which a standing army embodied. They learned, for the first time, how necessary it is that the civil should control the military.

Their second lesson came about forty years later under James II. A rebellion by the Duke of Monmouth had been made an excuse for a large increase in the standing army. When James II came to the throne he demanded more troops and Parliament refused him. Their fear of a standing army was greater than their loyalty to the King. Nevertheless, James was able to use his army to intimidate the courts and to make them entirely subservient to his will, to destroy academic freedom in Oxford University and to attempt, although with less success, to destroy it at Cambridge. But what was most terrifying of all, he used the threat represented by the standing army to attempt to impose religious views and opinions. For this latter, especially, his people never forgave him, and ultimately they overthrew him. The lesson embodied in this entire affair was one of the principal political maxims which the colonists carried across the sea, and the maxim was: "Standing armies always threaten civil liberties."

There was a third historical memory which the colonists never relinquished and that was the famous "Popish Plot" which occurred during the reign of Charles II, in 1678 to be exact. This whole plot demonstrated an extremely unsavory condition which existed in late seventeenth-century England: the reliance of the government on paid political informers, that is, men who, for money, reported to the authorities their suspicions, conjectures or facts about other men whose political views were considered unreliable.

This plot was the invention of such a paid political informer, Titus Oates, who was, says the historian J. R. Green, "One of those vile imposters who are always thrown to the surface at times of great public agitation." The instability of this man's personality is shown by the fact that he was initially a Baptist minister who became a Catholic convert. He entered a Jesuit house and was expelled for misconduct. He thereupon made an affidavit saying that the Catholics were going to kill King Charles II and subvert the Protestant religion in England. This was heady stuff, and those who wished to believe it promptly did so. The entire nation might not have been too excited if it had not been for the remarkable slaying of Sir Edmondsbury Godfrey, the magistrate before whom Oates had given his information. This magistrate was found in a field near London with a sword run through his heart by some person or persons unknown. A panic ensued, and with it there came a total suspension of civil liberties for a substantial minority of the English nation. Two thousand Catholics were placed in prison, and a proclamation ordered every Catholic to leave London. This extraordinary abrogation of civil rights probably has no parallel until 1941 when the United States government excluded the Japanese from the West Coast. The Commanding General's final report referred to all individuals of Japanese descent as "subversive" as belonging to "an enemy race" whose "racial strains are undiluted." So it was in seventeenth-century England. An exclusion bill was passed in Parliament which prohibited any Catholic from holding a seat in either house of Parliament, and this bill remained in force for over a century and a half.

But soon this plot began to wane, as plots based on hysteria rather than fact inevitably must. Suspicions concerning the reality of the plot were voiced in Parliament, and so the government did a remarkable thing. It offered a reward for anyone coming forward with evidence to support the plot. A man named Bedloe came forward and took the money. In exchange for it he swore to knowledge of a plot for the landing of a Catholic army which was to engage in a general massacre of Protestant civilians. Naturally Titus Oates felt the need to restore his own position as chief informer. Consequently he charged the Queen with intent to murder her husband. I thought that hysteria and falsehood could scarcely go further until I read, recently, of a group in Phoenix who have charged Senator Goldwater with being a Communist and then I felt that I knew what my own English ancestors must once have felt and thought.

As a result of this new information a proclamation enjoined the arrest of every Catholic in the realm, and then a series of judicial murders began which soon horrified the conscience of the English people and brought them to their senses. Then there ensued a revulsion against the whole device of paid informers and political police that left a mark on the literature as well as the laws of the eighteenth century. For example Jonathan Swift, in the first book of *Gulliver's Travels,* tells us that the people of Lilliput have fortified their state against informers. If a man is accused falsely of a crime against the state, his accuser is to be put to death immediately. The lands and goods of the false accuser are then to be sold and the proceeds given to the one falsely accused.

And so the framers of our Constitution carefully worked safeguards into the Bill of Rights and into our legal system in order that the abuses to which political police and paid informers are so peculiarly subject, might be avoided and the individual protected. It is well to remind ourselves, first of the abuse of civil liberties embodied in paid informers and political police, and then of the safeguards which were devised. First, the political informer may often be an unstable personality given to fanaticism and excess. Second, such a person, led by a profit motive, may completely ignore the rules of fair play and the spirit of the due process of law. Finally, the charges of such persons may prove extremely useful to demagogues and extremely dangerous to minorities.

The safeguards, if observed, were adequate. There are actually many more provisions than I shall name, but four of them seem to be particularly important.

1. No one is to be punished unless his conduct is in violation of a law in force at the time his acts are committed. *Ex post facto* laws are incompatible with civil liberties.

2. The accused must, as the most elementary demand of justice, be apprised of the nature of the charge made against him and the identity of his accuser.

3. The accused must be allowed to confront his accuser in open court, to examine the accuser, witnesses and materials used against him. If there are reluctant witnesses, the court may use its authority to bring them in.

4. Finally, there is a presumption of innocence until proof of guilt is established by due process of law, not by suspicion, not by hysteria, not by association, not by prejudice but by due process of the fullness of justice and the majesty of law.

And so if I may conclude this historical excursion, I would affirm without hesitation that the two most potent fears of the Colonial American were his fear of a standing army and his fear of the abrogation of the due process of law. It remains to be seen how we, the descendants of that American, have managed to preserve and foster the safeguards he erected against these fears.

With the kind of background which I have presented, I should now like to examine the two military systems that faced one another in the Revolutionary War. The British Army had long since lost the vision of the freeman who had left the plow to take up the bow. It was officered by the younger sons of noble or wealthy families who had purchased their commissions. The enlisted men could roughly be divided into two groups. The first were the mercenaries upon whom American romanticism has poured so much scorn. They were men, for the most part, who chose a military career because none better was open to them and they proved, in many engagements, to be superior to volunteers, as professionals are always better than amateurs. The other enlisted men constituted the Royal Army, the standing army which the colonists refused to have in America, the professional long-service soldiers and seamen who could be hired, threatened or impressed into doing the nation's fighting.

The Americans who faced them were Colonial citizens. Many of them had served in their local militias. As is well known, the Massachusetts colony resorted to the famous device of the Minute Men. The youngest and most active on the militia rolls were placed in special companies to be ready at a minute's notice; the more sedentary warriors were consigned to "alarm companies," to be used only if things were truly alarming.

Note the irony here. The American forces embodied the old British dream of the yeoman landholder resisting invasion; the British, on the other hand, with their "lobsterbacks" or redcoats, embodied the idea of the professional army. And so if dreams come true, we should easily have won. But the fact is that the British had a real advantage that Washington was soon to discover. Their professional force was enlisted for a long period of service; the Colonials on the other hand were volunteers who had enlisted only for the "campaign." That meant the summer fighting season and their terms were scheduled to run out at the end of the year. The congressional committee which reviewed this alarming situation assumed that it could get these troops to re-enlist. It was never more mistaken. The troops went home as their terms ran out, and often took with them the muskets and equipment so desperately needed. This is what Hamilton meant when he said that our fear of a professional army had almost cost us our liberty. And this led Washington to formulate a new philosophy concerning military service. He spoke of the "extraordinary and reprehensible conduct" of these men who went home when their enlistment was up without further regard to the safety of the nation. Toward the end of the war he asked for a regular long-service army, like that of the British, and larger enlistment bonuses on the grounds that "interest" and not "patriotism" could bring men to serve for the long pull. He noted further that the original passion for liberty seemed to have faded and that self-interest remained the only motive to which the state could appeal in securing the duty of its citizens. The dream of the yeoman-soldier was already slightly tarnished.

General Washington said one other thing which was portentous for the future. Shortly after taking command in 1775, he was presented with the case of an officer who wished to resign his commission because he believed that he had not been given sufficient rank. Washington wrote him:

> In the usual contests of Empire and Ambition, the conscience of a soldier has so little share that he may very properly insist upon his claims of Rank . . . but in such a cause as this where the Object is neither Glory nor extent of territory, but a defense of all that is dear and valuable in Life surely every post ought to be deemed honorable in which a Man can serve his Country.

The British regular, in other words, fought for empire; the Colonial citizen for "all that was dear and valuable in life." If this were so, then surely the state had a military claim on every citizen. The whole democratization of war is implicit in Washington's statement and that democratization, the total claim of the state upon its citizens for military service, is now with us. Universal Military Training is the logical result of Washington's position.

There is certainly one good side to this which we might mention in passing. The citizen who has served his country in order to defend all that is dear and valuable in life has a claim upon the state. And to this fact a number of veterans' benefits may be traced such as the GI Bill or free hospitalization for veterans who have service-incurred disabilities. But even more important, the service rendered by the Japanese and Negro citizens in World War II and in the Korean war gave them inescapable claims upon the state. I personally consider this far more important than anything the courts have done in the elimination of racial discriminations.

There now begins a pattern in American military affairs which I would like to trace out. First the American people historically rejected Hamilton's plea for a professional army and tried to get by with militia. These militia could not be used for foreign adventures but only to "repel invasion." Further their enlistment period was for three months only. The disaster suffered by Arnold and Montgomery at Quebec on December 31, 1775, was largely owing to the fact that they had to engage battle before they were ready in order not to lose their troops whose time was to expire the next day on January 1. Again at the end of 1776, because their enlistment was up, Washington lost almost all of his troops and had to build a new army in the face of the enemy.

During the War of 1812, the British were attempting to take New Orleans. The federal government, with no army of its own, called upon the states for their militiamen. Massachusetts attempted to refuse on the ground that her troops could only be called to repel invasion and that Massachusetts was not being invaded. The governor of Vermont sent his regrets with the same excuse. During the Mexican War in 1845, Zachary Taylor got 10,000 militiamen from Louisiana and Texas. When their three months were up they left him. General Winfield Scott, in 1847, came to know firsthand what General Washington had once undergone. When he climbed to the plateau of Mexico and began to ready the final battle, his volunteer units went home, and he had to suspend operations until they could be replaced. The green and untried replacements ultimately suffered heavy losses.

This pattern continued during the Civil War. The Volunteer Corps of 75,000 men went home after three months. New York's 7th Regiment went home immediately after the Battle of Bull Run, not because they were cowards but because their time was up, just as I came home from Korea in 1952 because I had served my hitch.

Then came World War I and the Americans still refused to abandon the militia or volunteer system. And by now this refusal was becoming dangerous. Both France and Germany kept some 800,000 men in their armies in peacetime. When mobilization was complete, the Germans had 1,750,000 men in the field. And so military men began to ask if we should not democratize war in America, make it the duty of every able-bodied man. In 1914, Wilson replied in the negative:

It is said in some quarters that we are not prepared for war. What is meant by being prepared? Is it meant that we are not ready upon brief notice to put a nation in the field, a nation of men trained to arms? Of course we are not ready to do that; and we shall never be in time of peace so long as we retain our present political principles and institutions.

He then continued in the language of the old American dream, the dream of the yeoman-farmer and his squirrel rifle:

We must depend in every time of national peril not upon a standing army nor yet a reserve army, but upon a citizenry trained and accustomed to arms. . . .

On June 3, 1916, there was a National Defense Act. Thirteen days later, the entire National Guard of the United States was called out under its provisions, and for the *first time* in American military history, they came not as three-months' volunteers who could only repel invasion, nor as volunteers serving a limited term, but as conscripts obligated to accept whatever duties and obligations the federal government should demand of them.

In a few months, the Defense Act was scrapped and a draft act was passed. "It is a new thing in our history," said President Wilson, "and a landmark in our progress." He continued in words that some of the draftees might have hooted at, "It is in no sense a conscription of the unwilling; it is, rather, a selection from a nation which has volunteered in mass."

Was this a landmark in our progress? Well, sadly enough, it probably was, if war were to be the permanent condition. But what of our long history of fierce defense of civil liberties against the threat of standing armies? Faced with the Kaiser's armies, the American people simply did not talk about it. They broke a long and honorable historical pattern because they thought they had to. And let it be a part of the record that the intervention of our armies did avert the defeat of the British and French and assured for a short time (how pitifully short!) the ascendance of the democratic world.

I have traced out one long historical pattern and the breaking of that pattern in the face of war. Let me now trace out another one and its ultimate end. After every bitter experience of the untrained militia and the short-term volunteers, the leaders of the nation tried to get the people to permit them to maintain a small trained army during peacetime. After the Revolution, Hamilton said, "Altho' a *large* standing Army in time of Peace hath ever been considered dangerous to the liberties of a Country, yet a few Troops, under certain circumstances, are not only safe, but indispensably necessary." He then asked for four regiments of infantry and one of artillery or 2,631 men in all. Congress then debated the issue, and on June 2, 1784, it directed the discharge of all troops in the service of the United States except for "twenty-five privates to guard the stores at Fort Pitt and fifty-five to guard the stores at West Point, with a proportionate number of officers," none of whom was to be above the rank of captain. The Congress concluded with what might be called, until recent times, the principal American military axiom: "Standing armies in time of peace are inconsistent with the principles of republican governments."

After the War of 1812, the Congress immediately reduced the army from 38,000 to 10,000 men and in 1820 ordered the Secretary of War to cut it down to 6,000. The cut was made, but not even this force could be maintained because enlistments dwindled. This fact pleased William H. Sumner, who wrote to President John Adams in 1823, "The militia is intended for defense only; standing armies for aggression as well as defense. The history of all ages proves that large armies are dangerous to civil liberties."

This pattern continued after the Mexican War and the Civil War. In the first year the latter ended, a million men were mustered out. By 1869, the national army consisted of only 25,000 men, and it remained at approximately that strength until the Spanish American War. After World War I, even the pacifistic Wilson was inclined to think that we should maintain a standing army of some size. But the Congress noted that there had been over 11,000 desertions by NCO's and enlisted men from the regular army not to mention the regular resignations. By 1927 the standing army had dwindled to 120,000 men.

Again after World War II, there was a rush to disarm. Some blamed this on Communist agitation, and quite likely there was some of that. But the hurry to leave when war is over is a long-established American historical pattern. No Communist ever talked to me, and I could not wait to get home. In any case by 1948 our 13 million troops had shrunk to 1,374,000. In 1948 the military men quite justifiably alarmed, in my opinion, considering the state of the world, asked for Universal Military Training. Congress, following its historical pattern, refused to grant it but did re-enact Selective Service, and, fearful of a large military establishment, placed a ceiling of 15 billion on military expenditures. By 1950 the Korean War was on, and the ceiling was lifted to 60 billion where it has remained ever since. When the Korean War was over, we broke our historical pattern by not demobilizing and by making no cutbacks in military expenditure. In 1951 the Universal Military Training and Service Act was passed. Technically we were not at war and this was then universal peacetime conscription. The Reserve Act of 1955 continues this state of affairs.

I hope it is clear that I am not blaming anyone for all of this. We have had enough loose talk about plots and evil motives without my adding to it. I have tried to show that an open society, fiercely proud of its civil liberties, finally, in the face of external military power and in the face of a great fear which that power engendered, gradually broke many of its own historical patterns concerning the role and function of the military, especially in peacetime.

Again and again we have heard our nation's leaders say, "This is something new in our history." And it is this very newness, this lack of experience in living with new conditions, this very uncertainty of trying to establish new patterns in place of broken ones that justifiably makes us all apprehensive. This, let me repeat, is the principal danger:

the establishment of a new source of overwhelming power at the same time in which we have destroyed the historical patterns which have hitherto controlled this power.

First, let us look for a moment at the size of the monster we have made. Last year we collected 78 billion dollars in federal taxes. Of this amount, 46 billion went into defense outlays; veterans' benefits took 5 billion and the interest on the national debt, which is largely a result of military expenditure, was 9 billion. Perhaps we should add to this 2 billion dollars for foreign aid, and we have the total cost of making war or being prepared to make war. It adds up to 62 billion out of the total of 78 billion, or about 80 per cent of our total federal budget.

Let us see what this means in terms of science. From 1955 until 1959 we spent about 2 billion for scientific research. About 120 million, or 6 per cent, went into basic research. Nearly all of the rest went into military technology.

In addition to these vast expenditures, we are keeping about three million men in uniform. To keep the ranks filled we have laid an eight-year military obligation on all young American males.

Industrial corporations have grown proportionately. Of the total military budget of 1961, some 21 billion was spent on procurement. About three-fourths of this staggering total went to 100 corporations. Three corporations got more than a billion each. General Dynamics received 1.26 billion; Lockheed and Boeing each received slightly more than 1 billion. General Electric and North American Aviation received just under 1 billion.

Please keep in mind that 86.4 per cent of this total was awarded without competitive bidding. So the question naturally arises of influence peddling, of a combine of military-industrial power. The Hebert Investigating Committee in 1959-60 found that more than 1400 retired officers were employed by the top hundred corporations which spent three-fourths of the 21 billion. There were 261 generals or admirals among them. General Dynamics, the corporation that received the largest amount of defense money, also had the largest number of retired officers on its payroll, 187 to be exact, including 27 generals and admirals.

Please understand that I am not making any accusations or even insinuations. I simply point to a dubious situation which we have not yet come to grips with. Surely, all this can make us sympathize with the statement issued by that staunch New Englander, Senator Ralph E. Flanders, Republican of Vermont:

It is not only that we are sacrificing to defense our standard of living and the free independence of our economic life, we are sacrificing our freedom itself. We are being forced to shift the American way of life into the pattern of the garrison state.

I have tried to trace the gradual relinquishment of the dream of an armed citizenry more jealous of its civil liberties than fearful of foreign tyranny, a dream that has gradually and unavoidably faded under the increasing threat of foreign enemies. I have tried to show something new among us, a shift of power so immense, so demanding on our national economy and energy, so all-encompassing in its universal claim on our lives, our loyalties, and our liberties that we must at least alert ourselves to the area of danger and try to minimize as best we can the inherent threats to our freedom.

First I should like to take up the problem of the political police. Prolonged international tension provides the rationale for the existence of a political police force, the FBI. That sedition and subversion must be controlled is not, in my judgment, open to question. But unfortunately they cannot be controlled without the use of self-incrimination, condemnation by association, without tests for utterance or received opinion. As Walter Millis has said, "Disloyalty or sedition are matters of the inner mind and emotions, and these are accessible to the investigator in no other way." And so the government agencies, on numerous occasions, have asked for a prosecution of American citizens, but have been reluctant to produce the accusers in open court or to allow defense counsel to examine the evidence and testimony on which charges were based. The reason for acting in this way was a perfectly logical one. The FBI relies heavily on a system of paid informers. If the identity of these people is disclosed, their usefulness in preventing subversion or sedition is at an end. But if their identity is not disclosed, there results a serious infringement on the rights of individuals, the door is opened to all kinds of abuses, and the entire spirit of the due process of law is compromised.

Naturally the courts sooner or later had to meet this problem and, in a number of important decisions, Parker vs. Lester (Ninth Circuit Court of Appeals) and in the Supreme Court cases of Sweezy, Watkins and Jencks, our federal judges weighed the extremely critical matter of national security against the extremely critical matter of individual rights. In the Jencks case, they informed the Justice Department, in effect, that they must, if they intended to prosecute, make an open confrontation of accuser and accused in court, that the defense must be able to examine witnesses, and that previous statements of informers (presumably available only in secret files of the FBI) must be made available to the defense. In other words, the courts, in effect, said to the governmental agencies charged with protecting us against subversion, "You must decide whether you will prosecute and by so doing open your files and reveal your sources of information, or whether you will protect those sources and allow a suspected subversive to continue to go free."

Surely no one will deny that this was a real dilemma, that the requirements of due process hamper the work of our political police in a way that it does not hamper the political police of the Communist state. And so it is not surprising that it was these very decisions, made with a painful awareness of the perils to freedom both from political subversion and from failure to observe due process, that led to the formation of certain private and voluntary political police associations which, without official knowledge or concurrence, and without observing any of the safeguards of due process, collect dossiers on various American citizens and circulate these dossiers sometimes quite indiscriminately to employers, superiors, or associates. Generally this is done without observing the most elementary decency of informing the person in question that he is being accused.

The people engaged in this ugly business appear to believe quite sincerely that they are good Americans fostering the liberties of this nation. But it is a radically new and menacing development in American life. For centuries it has been known in many lands and under many governments where the people had no adequate protection of the laws. But like Universal Military Training, like standing armies in peacetime, it is something new with us. It is an ancillary development of the garrison state and we ought to oppose it.

The second great point of danger to our liberties as a result of the rise of the garrison state is the massive involvement of the military in domestic politics. Again this is something entirely new, such a radical departure from our historical traditions that I am unable to understand why Americans are not outraged by it.

All over the nation, military commanders are presiding at "seminars" which involve the political indoctrination of civilians. One military commander, General Walker, an admitted member of the John Birch society, tried to influence the voting of his troops. Lieutenant Stephen Huffaker, a native Salt Laker, while in the service gave speeches to more than 60 groups in California. He said, among other things, that his listeners must not believe the American press because it was pro-Communist. It should be noted in passing that Lieutenant Huffaker had previously worked for the *Deseret News* and therefore presumably knew at first hand what he was talking about. And he asked these questions: "Do you want federal aid to education? Do you want federal aid to churches? Do you want socialism?" In other words, he equated a part of the domestic program of this and previous administrations with communism.

Senator Strom Thurmond, who fanatically defends this new role of the military in our national life, has recognized clearly that the military is engaged in domestic politics, and he is willing to uphold such engagement. Senator Thurmond himself, incidentally, is a general in the Reserve and stated:

> If the military teaches the true nature of communism, it must necessarily teach that communism is fundamentally socialism. When socialism, in turn, is understood, one cannot help but realize that many of the domestic programs advocated in the United States and many of those adopted, fall clearly within the category of socialism.

The conclusion is inescapable. Senator Thurmond sees it as the duty of the military to indoctrinate the public in domestic politics. Our founding fathers would have turned over in their graves.

In military-sponsored seminars in Pensacola; San Antonio; Glenview, Illinois; Houston and Corpus Christi, Texas; as well as other places, right-wing speakers have implied that General George C. Marshall and President Harry Truman were traitors and that those who support the programs and policies of the Eisenhower and Kennedy administrations are either pro-Communists or Communist dupes.

To my mind, this involvement of the military in domestic politics is the clearest immediate danger that the vast military establishment poses. How far are we from the situation in Algeria where the French military are engaged in a mutiny against their legal government? I think that we are quite far, and I hope we are, but I also recall that the revolt of the Military Brass against the current attempts of Secretary McNamara to establish authoritatively the civilian supremacy over the military was referred to by Senator Stuart Symington, himself one of our chief advocates of military preparedness, as "a disloyal operation." Those are ugly words; I hope that they are not true. But of one thing I am sure. The military establishment has no business in domestic politics; it never did; it never will. And the time is now for the kind of emphatic, precedent-setting expression of the national will which will check this one dangerous overflow of power into an area of the national life which has hitherto successfully resisted it.

I should like to point up a profound irony here. Our English and Colonial forefathers feared a standing army because they thought that it could be used to execute the will of a tyrant and deprive citizens of their liberties. But the real danger now is that the military establishment will unite, not with a tyrant, but with the masses, with an irrational political Third Estate. It is the people who threaten the liberties of the people.

Let me define the term "Third Estate." It originally meant the third of the three classes of people whose consent was necessary for legislation: the nobles, the clergy, and the commons. The commons, in those ancient and desperate times, were not often moved by reason; they were subject to hungers and fears; they understood best what we would call "belly politics." Their desperations, their irrationalities, their failure to pursue principle or policy, and their dogged adherence to their emotional proclivities often earned the contempt of the nobles and the mistrust of the clergy.

We are often misinformed about the extent of the Third Estate among us today. *Life* magazine noted with some surprise a few years ago that there may be as high as 14 million members of the religious third estate in America, those who are not members of any of the major churches, but who belong, rather, to pentecostal groups who speak in tongues, who thirst for revivalism, who demand the strong wine of miracle and ecstasy, of doom and gore, of cosmic threat and cosmic assurance. And although the boundaries shift, there is also a political third estate, a group profoundly alienated from the major parties, from the traditional patterns, and from the historical context of the nation. Among these people there is a high degree of frustration, a readiness to hate, a hunger for scapegoats and sacrificial enemies, a need for the kind of certainty and assurance that only oversimplification can give. At the moment, elements of the military establishment are fervently allied with this political third estate. And there, at the moment, lies the second real danger which we confront as a result of our large military establishment.

I should like to make a little further analysis of our political third estate. The philosophers of existentialism have acquainted us with a new phrase, "existential anxiety." This existential anxiety they distinguish from ordinary fear. Fear, they say, has an object or an apparent cause. We may fear disease or impotence or especially we may fear death as we discover how brief a moment we have in the sun before we shall all "lie down in darkness."

Existential anxiety is distinguished from ordinary fear by the fact that it has no apparent object or cause. Or at least we could say this, the sum of our anxiety and fear is greater than the sum of the objects or causes which produce that anxiety. But, unfortunately, it takes a certain intellectual sophistication to grasp such an idea. For people of the Third Estate, fear is very real; and if fear exists there must be a cause, an object, a reason. And so objects are sought. Now if one were to determine that the chief object of his anxiety were Russia, he might, without being a neurotic, decide to hate Russia, unless of course, by some chance he were a Christian. Then he would need to look for a different solution. But more neurotic solutions would be to find the enemy, not three thousand miles away, but all around you, in the same church, the same school, the same family. We are close to paranoia here as everyone must surely recognize, and it is the people who have adopted this neurotic solution with whom an important segment of the military establishment has chosen to ally itself at this critical moment in our history.

I have pointed out two areas of danger: the rise of political police activity and the involvement of the military in domestic politics. Now I should like to suggest two areas of activity which I think we very much need to strengthen. I cannot, at this time, undertake to say how it will or ought to be done. I shall merely express my feeling that these are directions in which we need to go.

First, I should like to see us encourage and strengthen the religious element in our culture which is generally called the "prophetic" element, that element which stresses the fatherhood of God and the brotherhood of man; which is wise, tolerant, committed to human and social values and which refuses to accept hatred and total annihilation as the means and end of human endeavor. America has frequently been moved by leaders of the religious third estate: Billy Sunday or Amy Semple McPherson, but, as a nation, we have never known what it is to have a living image of a prophetic religion comparable to that which Ghandi provided for the Hindus or Martin Buber for the Jews or Albert Schweitzer for German Protestants. I believe that the religious people of this nation would respond to a sane, kindly, decent and devoted religious leadership which would show us as immediately and as intimately as Ghandi showed his Hindu contemporaries the beauty of holiness, the power of love, and the impotence of hate.

Second, I should like to see a recrudescence of the old Puritan virtues. I think I know as well as any man the limitations of the Puritans and the many failures in their character and society. But they held basically to one terrible and magnificent tenet: the individual's responsibility to his own conscience. And with it there went a sense of vocation, of calling, of stewardship, a feeling that he was engaged in a life fraught with great meaning and that it became him to acquit himself well. It is a slackening in our moral fibre that disturbs me: the high incidence of crime and juvenile delinquency; racketeering in the labor unions; price-fixing in business; payola; the Madison Avenue complex; corruption and greed; the gradual acceptance of the most hideous forms of violence, a gradual acquiescence in the total demands of the garrison state.

We need a rededication to humane values, to moral and ethical living. I wish that some Ghandi would arise to lead us, but I suspect that he will not. But there is still left for each of us the course of action recommended in an old proverb that came from one of the wisest peoples the world has produced, the Jews. There is an old Rabbinic proverb which says, "Is there need of a man? Be thou *that* man."

Comments

RICHARD B. KREUTZER

Dean Adamson has very capably covered the historical roots of the American antipathy toward the military which basically stemmed from European experiences. It might be noted in passing that jealousies among the original states and their unfounded fears of a strong federal government were also factors. In retrospect it seems somewhat incongruous that such a feeling would perpetuate itself in spite of the fact that our armed forces have proven time and again their dedication to our country's democratic principles. Their record of noninvolvement in domestic politics over the past 186 years has been unique among the histories of the various nations included in a "great power" status.

I can only reinforce Dean Adamson's analysis of the inadequacies of our traditional reliance on the militia-type armies. This theory plus the specter of militarism plus the recurrent cry for "economy as an over-riding consideration" has been largely responsible for our unpreparedness in *all* of the *eight* major wars in which we have engaged. These attitudes, singly or in combination, have resulted in the unnecessary loss of many lives, not to mention the possibility of outright defeat in the initial phases of several of these conflicts.

Although the outlawing of war by general disarmament, under adequate controls, may become an eventual reality, we must not be placed in a position of serious military disadvantage until it does. Today we are faced with tremendous international responsibilities which under the present conditions of tension and distrust require an adequate and modern force-in-being. In addition, within the ranges of the possible spectrum of involvement, we require substantial reserves which are highly trained in the complexities of modern warfare and are available on short notice. The day and age of "musket or pitchfork" military preparedness philosophy is gone forever. The size and composition of our armed forces are based on recommendations of our military professionals and approved by the civilian representatives of the executive branch of our government, closely monitored by the legislative branch. From all evidence to date every effort is being made to keep the size of our armed forces to a minimum consistent with our world-wide political commitments.

It may be somewhat enlightening at this point to review the various elements which might be included as being a part of the rather generic term "the military establishment." First, there is the active army composed of our professional cadre and of citizen-soldiers on active duty for varying lengths of service. These individuals are responsible to the federal authorities for duty assignments and for their actions. Closely allied to this group are the retirees who have completed their required active duty service of either twenty or thirty years. Retired personnel are in fact civilians with the rights and privileges thereof. Still another broad category are the reservists — National Guardsmen, and other reserve forces for the active army. The National Guardsmen are directly responsible to the state governments; however, they retain their individual status as full-fledged civilians. The remaining members of our reserve forces are civilians with obligations for periodic attendance at training sessions. Thus, it should be understood that when an *individual* affiliated with our military establishment, using the term in the context just discussed — when such an individual speaks or acts, he may be speaking or acting as an ordinary citizen, as an agent of a state government, or as a representative of the federal government.

Before commenting on certain of Dr. Adamson's specific points, I should like to mention several general propositions which are universally accepted in American military circles:

I am sure all of us would agree without reservation to the general proposition which subordinates the military to civilian control in our governmental structure.

There should be no question as to the propriety of active duty personnel involving themselves in partisan domestic politics, or for that matter, in controversial international political affairs without clearance from their civilian superiors. These actions should *not* be condoned.

When speaking to the general public on issues involving governmental matters in which they are competent to speak, military personnel should stay within established administration policy.

As in the academic field of endeavor, military personnel should be encouraged to develop and publish ideas which will stimulate professional growth. They also should be encouraged honestly and forcefully to present their professional opinions to their civilian superiors or when appearing as witnesses in congressional hearings.

Lastly, military commanders must ensure that their troops are physically and psychologically prepared for possible combat operations.

Now with the foregoing remarks as a backdrop, permit me to elaborate on a few of Dean Adamson's specific comments relating to the involvement of military personnel in domestic affairs.

First, with regard to the employment of retired military personnel by business firms — the majority of these individuals are highly trained in both technical and managerial activities. It is inconceivable to me that after thirty years of devoted duty to their country, as a group they would place economic gain ahead of the welfare of their nation. It should be mentioned that the fourteen hundred military-businessmen are only a very small proportion of the tens of thousands of retired personnel who are presently actively engaged in various civic activities throughout our nation. To mention only a few outstanding examples: General Alfred Gruenther, chairman of the American Red Cross; General Troy Middleton, president of Louisiana State University; General J. C. H. Lee, president, Episcopal Laymen Society of U.S.: General James Gavin, ambassador to France; and, of course, General Dwight Eisenhower.

Now a few words about the military-sponsored seminars Dean Adamson mentioned. In 1958 the National Security Council directed the Department of Defense to conduct annual seminars for selected reserve officers for the purposes of (and I quote from the syllabus of the National War College, which conducted these seminars):

First — to provide a selected group of reserve officers with a better understanding of the world conflict and of the organization, resources and methods used by the adversaries to accomplish their aims.

Second — to alert these selected leaders to the threat posed by, and the dangers of, the cold war, as well as to inform them of U.S. plans and programs in support of national security policy.

Third — to present to this group ideas and programs for creating a resolute and informed U.S. climate of opinion and to inspire them to help create, through their positions as leaders in civilian life, a determined national will to resist Communist strategems and to support national security programs.

The bulk of the curriculum was prepared by the Foreign Policy Research Institute of the University of Pennsylvania. Attending these seminars were civilian leaders from all over the United States — lawyers, ministers, businessmen, editors and educators. At the 1961 seminar there were forty-six civilian educators of whom three were college presidents and four were college deans. Again, it should be emphasized that these seminars were directed by the highest civilian authorities in our governmental structure.

In the last decade there has been tremendous progress made in the unification of our armed forces and in the co-operation between the civilian and military members of the defense establishment. Granted, it has been a rocky road, sometimes partially blocked by personalities and old prejudices. However, today there is close co-operation among the services and in the Department of Defense. Much of this progress has been due to capable, energetic and positive leadership on the part of the civilian directors of the defense effort — an indispensable ingredient for success in this area.

I see no basis for comparison of the present French army difficulties in Algeria with the present status of our armed forces. I am confident that our armed forces, built primarily upon the moral foundation which is the basis of our Constitution, will never usurp the prerogatives of the duly elected representatives of the people. It would seem to me the Civil War fixed the basic solidarity of both our government and of our armed forces.

Lastly, as far as I know — and I have seen no documentary proof to the contrary — there is little validity in the allegation that elements of the *active duty* military forces (excepting a possible individual case) are allied to the "so called" political third estate. I suspect that such an association may be due to misinterpretation of the military's strong inherent concern for the nation's security.

In conclusion, I would add one area of concern to those Dean Adamson mentioned at the end of his talk. The time has come to return to the kind of devotion to our country which was evidenced by George Washington during the dark days of Valley Forge and by others of our early American leaders. They recognized that the foundation of our individual freedoms and liberty is based to a large extent on the confidence of the American people in the strength and stability of our governmental institutions which includes our armed forces.

OBERT C. TANNER

Dean Adamson points out that presently the military is a danger to our freedoms because of its size and influence. He states that within the past eight years this country has been changed into something like a garrison state. This has come about by combining the military with large segments of our corporate industrial life. Added to this, military leaders are now influencing local politics. Finally, there is a growing unification of an irrational political third estate, with some elements of our military.

His paper is one that should be read by every American. It is a review of how freedoms are lost to a giant combine of great power. I find no fault with his facts and no flaw in his conclusion.

So I would like to turn to another facet of the problem of freedom and the military.

I would like first to state that freedom at its very best is freedom to solve a problem; second, to spell out the great problem America is now trying to solve; third, to review the present military solution of this problem; and fourth, to indicate other ways freedoms can be used in the solution of this great problem.

First, what is freedom at its very best, on the highest possible level? It is the condition of a person or a nation that permits the use of *reason* in the solution of a problem.

There are many freedoms — freedom of the press, freedom of assembly, freedom of speech, but the highest use of freedom is the application of reason in solving a problem. Problems are solved by reason when there is a clear awareness of the problem needing a solution, careful observation of the actual situation, recognition of the various possible solutions based upon the available facts, collecting of more data relevant to the problem, and finally verification through trying out the proposed solution. A man or nation is truly free when there is freedom to apply this test of reason for solving problems. Stated negatively, a person or nation is not free to solve a problem by the application of freedom if there prevails: (*a*) a highly emotional state, such as fear or hate, and (*b*) if there is no open-minded humility that searches continually for more and more information — new facts, greater understanding.

Second, let us turn to the one great problem we hope America can solve successfully. Using our freedoms to live by reason, and applying the above method of reason, we must find ways whereby America can live in peace and *also* in freedom within the family of nations where a third of this family lies within the Communist bloc of nations.

Specifically, it is first, to live at peace under a threat that the Communist nations may start a war, and second, and even more difficult, it is to live in freedom when the Communist nations will try to infiltrate peacefully and thereby destroy all our freedoms without a war.

Stated in another way, how can America live in freedom and at peace with a billion people controlled by Communist leaders who are working every way they can for world domination?

Now if anybody can dream up a more difficult problem than this one, I would like to hear what it might be. And if anybody claims he knows a solution, he is kidding himself and I hope nobody else.

Third, the solution to this problem by America, this problem of communism, which is a problem of survival, and freedom if we survive, has been a solution any normal person or nation so threatened would naturally strive for. America has armed herself in self-defense. The solution of America to this problem of communism is a *military* solution. Our first obligation is to defend the life and freedom of this nation. Communist aggression now faces this new giant of our military establishment described by Dean Adamson, and for the protection afforded by this great military establishment, we are all justifiably thankful. The military may cost us some loss of freedoms — on a local level, as Dr. Adamson has accurately pointed out — but the military also insures a *greater* freedom on the international level — the very life of a free nation, which Dr. Adamson also points out as being absolutely necessary.

This brings me to my point: the military is necessary but not sufficient. While the military keeps watch, America must use *other* freedoms to solve this great problem of communism — solutions other than military. To this end I would establish four propositions:

1. America has never tried out nonmilitary solutions to any great extent.
2. Nonmilitary solutions require a nonmilitary frame of mind.
3. Nonmilitary solutions all aim toward the single goal of lessening international tension.
4. Our freedom should put the military in its proper place and reason in its proper place. If this can be done, America has a good chance of living at peace with freedom among neighbors, some of whom are communist neighbors.

America has not tried out nonmilitary solutions to the problem of communism because the military was a first and absolute necessity in facing Communist aggression. We have not had time to do much else but reach for our gun.

With the present size of the military and its absolute capability and even its vaster power of over-kill, we now at last have time to use our freedoms other than for military development. We now need a nonmilitary frame of mind.

This will require a vast shift in American psychology. In a single word, the demand now made upon every sober and responsible American is this: Have faith, grow in faith, develop your faith, search for a faith — in what? In the belief that we can find a nonmilitary solution to this Communist problem. Presently there is no such faith, or very little. Let it *not* be said by some celestial observer or some surviving historian of the southern hemisphere that America was lost to fall-out because her citizens had no faith in any solution but a military solution, and so war inevitably came.

The military frame of mind must not become the civilian frame of mind. If so, we are lost. The military psychology is necessarily such as to be ready for any eventuality — even sudden death. The civilian psychology must not be colored by this. No officer should talk to civilians as he would to the men of his command. Rather he shoud pray and hope with the men of his command that *we civilians* may be successful so that they — our soldiers and all our civilians too — may not perish. Survival now is not really a military issue. All that the military can do now is give us a little breathing spell to recover our rationality, to overcome our fears and escape our present ocean of hate and ill will.

The time has come now for us to cool off our emotions if we are to use reason. Emotions crowd reason to the wall and impale it there. While fully understanding the danger of communism and while firmly opposing it on every front, we must also preach love instead of hate, counsel wisdom instead of fear, publish more fairly the international news, support more fully the U.N., cast out news commentators who inflame rather than report, stop attending public gatherings of professional anti-Communists posing as experts while venting their spleen of hate and fear and ill-will — in short, American civilians and American military must part company in their frame of mind — the military psychologically ready for any possibility, and the civilians returning to our basic ideals of humaneness and fair play, even while dealing with our Communist neighbors.

Third, nonmilitary solutions to the communist problem are the same solutions nations have found successful in living at peace with one another in all ages past. These practices must now be applied toward the Communist nations: trade, cultural exchanges, tourist travel, shared support of the United Nations, patient diplomacy, and above all a careful regard by us for fact over fiction, for understanding over emotion, for patience over impulse, for humility over arrogance. Trade lessens international tension, as does travel and cultural exchanges. We risk nothing serious, if the military keeps watch, which it surely will do, while each American, each publisher, each politician, each teacher, each minister, each individual citizen searches out every way to lessen tension between the free and Communist worlds. Every word and act now has a single test: does it increase or decrease international tension? Does it lead in the direction of war or peace? This test must apply to every person's thinking and also to the policy of every organization in our great country.

Finally, we have now come to the opportune moment in history when the military must be relegated to a supporting role in American life. It must no longer play the lead in the center of the stage. This is the only hope for our country if we are to use our freedoms on the highest level — solving this most difficult problem by the application of a calm and careful reason, by searching out all the available facts, by some kind of sympathetic understanding of those we must vigorously oppose — in short, by a warm heart, an open mind, and a firm resolution to see our country through to a successful triumph, keeping both peace and our freedoms for generations to come.

③

Is Freedom of the Press Compatible With National Security?

NEAL A. MAXWELL

While our Constitution says Congress may make no law abridging freedom of the press, the existence of that prohibition does not guarantee access by the press to vital information, nor does it operate to require government to refrain from manipulating, distorting, withholding, or managing the news. Such practices usually occur in the name of national security and have, in the observation of America's most distinguished military editor, Hanson Baldwin, increased "markedly." Thus tonight's issue of compatibility is raised with urgency in a new and complex setting in which the aphorisms of Mill and Milton produce as much nostalgia as they do helpful guidance.

Like other freedoms, freedom of the press is in constant jeopardy, and it is susceptible to crass exploitation by a few irresponsibles who may profit personally or institutionally from the happy coincidence of this freedom and their own temporary interests. Risk and abuse are a part of the price we pay for a relatively open society; they are among the consequences of freedom.

Alongside our openness, there are, of course, competing rights and traditions favoring privacy in the home, the jury room, the judge's chamber and the voting booth. Our Constitution was produced in privacy.

Theorists have always assumed and argued, however, that a free press could check government by informing the citizenry and, therefore, we have accorded the press a privileged place even though it is a profit-making group. We have done this because in the words of Jefferson, though it is "chequered" with abuses, we are indebted to the press ". . . for *all* the triumphs over error and oppression." A case in point is the service of the British press during World War I, when it broke through censorship to report the poor handling of munitions in that nation's war effort. This performance was a factor in bringing about real improvements in Britain's war machinery through a change of government. But the press is always somewhat at the mercy of government. Prime Minister Baldwin observed in 1936 that ". . . democracy is always two years behind the dictator." Baldwin's "appalling" frankness on the

41

floor of Parliament in making this justification of his having deceived the British electorate as to the gravity of German rearmament rested upon the assumption that the people would not have rallied when confronted with the truth anyway, and that he would have thereby needlessly lost the election. How enticing to the sincerely concerned executive is this paternalistic path today!

The announced justification of censorship has always been to keep information of value from the enemy. Today, the body of information that could be regarded as falling into this category is strikingly large. The second reason for censorship — to keep from the public information which might adversely affect national morale — has been reinforced by new justifications which are to some fresh and compelling for keeping certain facts from the people.

Add to these modern conditions complexity itself, such as trying to report news about military technology or science, which T. S. Matthews says "comes to us more and more faintly, like the dwindling shouts of a search-party that has disappeared into an enormous maze," and one can then begin to appreciate how simple things were when it was enough to avoid the reporting of the sailing of a troop ship. Bertrand Russell sees this increased power that officials now have as a result of science as a ". . . behind-the-scenes power, like that of emperors' eunuchs and kings' mistresses in former times." This development places a premium upon interpretive news and therefore increases the need for newsmen and newspapers to alert the reader to their biases.

A further factor which mitigates against our traditional notion of full disclosure and discussion is the presence of persistent pessimism about public opinion. Apparently, the presentation of the NATO concept to Congress and the public was delayed for months because the people were thought unprepared for the program. Walter Lippmann bemoans this veto power of public opinion over decisions that officials who are "wiser" than the people might make, if they could. A veteran editor such as the *Times*' Baldwin is not optimistic about the capacity of our citizenry to maintain a prolonged posture of interest and understanding in public affairs, especially in such a scientific era. Yet, according to Francis L. Rourke in *Secrecy and Publicity*, C. P. Snow has argued that World War II might have ended sooner and with less cost if "secret politics" in Britian had not affected the conduct of the war.

A still further complication appears. Our open society publishes the persuasions and protests of men like Bertrand Russell, but there is no Soviet equivalent of Bertrand Russell marching and preaching in the streets of Moscow. Our open press of necessity exposes our people to the possibility of instantaneously induced fear, while no counterpart surge of emotion would necessarily exist on the Soviet side.

Finally, there is yet another new level of governmental secrecy: the emergence of policymaking at the United Nations, which affects American security. This body will often have its own institutional goals and military forces, and it seems inevitable that there will be occasions when the American public and even our government will be put in a posture of overdependence on the U. N. for information in matters affecting our national security.

Thus any examination of tonight's issue must take notice of all these factors and, finally, may turn on one's view of public opinion and, therefore, of human nature.

This paper will disappoint those, however, who see a "Gadianton" scheme of suppression on the part of officials who are ready to ring down a khaki curtain. It will also disappoint those who see a plot by a reckless press to spring sensitive, classified information and thereby jeopardize our national security.

Admittedly, there are a few reporters, such as the electronic journalists at the Little Rock crisis, who reportedly urged blacks and whites to mix it up for the television cameras so that there would be a little action. Such reporters compete journalistically only on the levels of speed and sensation.

There are also, unfortunately, some federal officials with the power to classify information in the interests of national security who cannot distinguish between withholding information about a road built with I.C.A. funds in Peru, started before the final route was selected and ended ignominiously at the foot of a mountain, and, on the other hand, withholding information on the whereabouts of a Polaris-armed nuclear sub on sea patrol. Such officials "transform procedure into purpose" and fail to understand the vital relationship between shared information and decision-making in a democracy and often harm the policy process even within the Executive itself. For instance, as Secretary of the Navy, James Forrestal was not "informed of this country's agreement with England not to use atomic weapons without mutual consent." He learned of this agreement only after he became Secretary of Defense and this then from two senators.

When, in 1787, Congress enacted a "housekeeping" statute it created what has since been referred to as "the fountainhead of secrecy," which authorized agency and department heads to set forth regulations concerning the custody, use and preservation of records, paper, and property. Although history reveals no congressional intent to provide for secrecy or the withholding of information, nevertheless, as the *Columbia Law Review* has pointed out, secrecy and claims of secrecy have been the result.

It is significant that over the years Congress has often been a provisional partner of the press — a role which must be noted in this paper — and has engaged in much ferreting, complaining, and cajoling about Executive practices which lessen the freedom of the press and restrict the flow of information. Congress sees secrecy as the "handmaiden of bureaucracy, especially military bureaucracy," yet it does much of its own work in secret.

Congress' own role relative to matters bearing on national security has, of course, declined in importance.

Katzenbach has noted how ". . . in time of peace prior to World War II Congress ordered the details of military legislation and made decisions for the Army and Navy quite as it did for the farmers, the businessmen, the fishermen, and others. It debated strategy and determined tactics. It digested the details of ship construction, the organization of artillery units. It advised the Army and Navy on the problems of command coordination and the cavalry on hay."

Today, as *Fortune Magazine* observed, ". . . Congressmen can really do little more than express general confidence or the lack of it in the management . . . the President and the Secretary of Defense can usually argue with the management only as laymen argue with professionals."

Legislators — as do pressmen — occasionally breach security. In 1941, Senator Burton K. Wheeler, an extreme isolationist, revealed the fact that the U.S. Navy was commencing its occupation of Iceland while that operation was underway and open to attack by Nazi submarines. Closer home, a member of the Utah congressional delegation revealed recently in the local press the actual production rate of Minuteman missiles by Hercules [Powder Company] in Utah each month, information which the Pentagon has classified as secret.

One wonders, for instance, what might have happened if there had been the press equivalent of Senator Fulbright's lonely but strong objections to the Cuban fiasco which he expressed privately to President Kennedy before its launching.

A good guide for today's contests between Congress and the press on the one hand and the Executive on the other is President Washington's response to the House effort to investigate the military disaster suffered by the forces of Major General St. Clair in 1791 in which the House asked for the files. Washington called a cabinet meeting in which it was decided that certain papers might be withheld for "the public good" at the President's discretion, but that, in this instance, all papers would be sent to the House. Freeman, Washington's biographer, says not even the "ugliest line" was eliminated because "Washington had learned long previously the protective value of candor in dealing with the American people and he knew that one reason for their trust in him was their belief he would tell them the whole truth." This was certainly in keeping with Milton's observation that ". . . when complaints are freely heard, deeply considered and speedily reformed, then is the utmost bound of civil liberty attained . . ." for ". . . errors in a good government and in a bad are equally almost incident."

A free press inevitably produces frustrations in society, especially in moments of crisis and obvious error. During the Cuban fiasco, the conduct of the American press apparently produced grave concern in President Kennedy and resulted in his desire to propose to publishers a kind of partnership-in-crisis.

Newspapers differed in handling stories dealing with the Cuban adventure. The *Saint Louis Post Dispatch* said in summation:

In the case of the Cuban affair, many newspapers of Florida agreed among themselves to say nothing about the training of refugees for the invasion. The *New York Times,* on the other hand, sent Latin American experts to Miami to obtain and publish as much information as they could obtain from refugee leaders. Obviously, the editors of the New York and Florida papers differed in their judgments, as was their right. It seems also obvious that if all the newspapers had agreed to conform to a code . . . the American people would be less able to evaluate the Cuban adventure and use its lessons to decide their future course. They might not have learned of the failure; they might not be in a position to demand an accounting.

One commentator said:

It would be better to conclude that maneuvers of this sort should not be undertaken by an open society than that our society should become less open.

The *London Times,* in reviewing examples of arguments for the press' entering into alliances with government, concluded that, "the first duty of the press is to obtain the earliest and most correct intelligence of the events of the time, and instantly, by disclosing them, to make them the common property of the nation." Lippmann has credited a paper he once edited, the *New York World,* with actually dissuading by sheer din our government from a military adventure in the twenties when there was real talk of our invading Mexico.

A probing press is no friend of officialdom during delicate negotiations either. In New Orleans in 1815, after the British were beaten, the *Louisiana Gazette* published a story about the conclusion of peace negotiations between the United States and England. General Andrew Jackson communicated with Godwin B. Cotten, editor of the *Gazette*, stating, "Henceforth it is expected that no publication in the nature of that hearing alluded to and censored will appear in any paper in this city unless the editor shall previously ascertain its correctness, and gain permission for its insertion from the proper source." When the editor protested, General Jackson imprisoned him. The incident was closed, however, when peace was officially proclaimed within a few days. What contribution the press could have made had it been even partially privy to diplomatic negotiations such as those at Yalta or to the serious deterioration of Soviet-American relations in the immediate post World War II period must be left to history. The point is that, although the presence of the press makes diplomacy more difficult, when the press has been excluded we have not automatically distinguished ourselves in diplomacy.

Voluntary suspensions of this traditional duel between the press and government have occurred, such as during the period of classic cooperation between government and the press in America in World War II. Editors were virtually their own censors, and a reporter like William Laurence of the *New York Times* was taken into the confidence of the government on the super-secret Manhattan project.

But such a suspension cannot safely be tolerated in a cold war that may run indefinitely, because the area of military concern is "constantly widening" and becoming ever more complex and inclusive.

The free press will and should, for these and many other reasons, resist the pleas of presidents and the Pentagon to "go responsible" or "to share in the labors of statesmanship." Freedom of the press is a tradition that demands a search beyond the news handout for the hidden. It is a tradition, which even more than our two-party system, will insure that a government will not be allowed the Orwellian opportunity to "reconcile contradictions" in order to retain power indefinitely. For it is only human for an official to feel that the journalists who do not promote his program are against him. Therefore, as an official becomes "encrusted with power," he often feels such reporters are actually working against the public interest, and hence he works against the press with an ironical sense of "public" purpose!

Veteran newsman Joseph Harsch put it succinctly when he said, ". . . there exists a built-in conflict between press and government . . . and this conflict is inevitable, desirable, and self-protecting." The government is "always seeking to increase its control over the flow of news and the good reporter is always pushing it back." History supports Harsch. Every president, including Jefferson, who spoke with such eloquence about the importance of newspapers, has withheld certain information from Congress and the press.

The irony of all this elaborate governmental effort at security is that although we have millions of documents classified as "secret," we actually have very few secrets. Production rates on military hardware are pretty well known from open sources, and so are the size and disposition of our military forces. Although American citizens ignore such news, Soviet agents do not.

One of the many reasons for senseless secrecy may be the basic attitudes toward freedom held by some in the military who deal with the press and who yield power to classify information. Almost symbolically, a United States Army Training Manual of 1928, defined democracy as:

The government of the masses. Authority derived from mass meetings or any other form of "direct" expression. Results in mobocracy. Attitude towards law is that the word of the majority shall regulate, whether it be based upon deliberation or governed by passion, prejudice, and impulse, without restraint or regard to consequences. Results in demagoguism, license, agitation, discontent, anarchy.[1]

This definition has been changed, of course, but there are fairly regular outcroppings in manuals and military publications today which suggest underlying attitudes which are ambivalent toward facets of our democracy. The attitude that reporters are "spies" and that "the public's thirst for news" can be likened to that "of a drunkard for brandy" did not die with the Civil War's General Sherman.

Often hostility to the press is the result of doting subordinates such as those who surrounded General Douglas MacArthur and who were anxious to protect him from what they regarded as the abuses of the press. A reporter who was frustrated in an attempt to cover an important conference between MacArthur and Hirohito concluded that the Japanese were not the only people with a peculiar idea of divinity in their leaders. Any such sense of "divinity," of course, can result in deception and distortion with regard to public information and the press must

---

[1] As quoted in "Essay on Liberty," volume 4, 1958. Published by the Foundation for Economic Education Incorporated, which cited United States Training Manual, No. 2000–25, 1928, p. 91.

retaliate iconoclastically. The book *The Conquered Press* said that during World War II, MacArthur's staff actually released communiques announcing the recapture of Clark Field days ahead of time but the censorship rule was "you cannot contradict the communiques."

The press itself has at times asked for military censorship, such as during the Korean War when correspondents were on their own for six months. This freedom lead to the application of diverse standards of reporting with many complaints from correspondents who felt their restraint had put them at the mercy of less responsible correspondents. This particular plea from the press had a Dostoevsky-like ring of "save us from ourselves," but it occurred.

Many silly and inconsistent practices by government in security matters have appeared which only add to the frustration of the public and the press and could be cited *ad nauseam!* For instance, the Army did not release its overseas base locations — which cannot be very well concealed — while the Navy and Air Force did. The Navy and the Army released the personnel strength overseas whereas the Air Force did not. Sometime ago the Air Force classified contracts for gas turbine engines whereas the Navy did not. General LeMay once refused to give certain figures regarding the B-52, only to learn that the then Secretary of Defense, Charles Wilson, later gave out figures on a television appearance. Still later the number of B-52's on hand, the planned monthly production rate, etc., were released. This particular attempt at secrecy was doomed at the outset anyway since the B-52's were numbered serially under the wings and could be easily observed moving across the road from the factory where they were produced to the field where they were temporarily kept.

In 1955 the Navy refused to clear for publication an article on the sinking of the *Indianapolis* during World War II on the grounds that it would reopen old wounds of the families of personnel who were lost, might adversely affect enlistments, and might also suggest the sinking of the *Indianapolis* was typical of the fate of other cruisers during World War II. The censor hopefully called attention to the fact that there were available many heroic stories of men on other cruisers who returned again to see their families.

Such examples bring to mind Josephus Daniels, World War I Secretary of the Navy, who observed that "God never made a man wise enough to be a censor."

As for managing the news, there is always the risk that government officials will use it for promotional purposes. One such case occurred in the fall of 1942 when an Army press agent revealed the "plot" by a rural fifth column to point out military objectives to enemy bombers by means of cunningly contrived groundmarkers. Much of the American press faithfully relayed the story to their readers in nearly 2000 news-papers. The story was not a deliberate fake, but it revealed "a fan-tastic miscarriage of information among Army air-men." The so-called markers on the eastern seaboard were investigated by the FBI, who con-cluded that the marks appeared to have been innocently made. Mean-while the pictures, without the results of the investigation, were for-warded to the First Air Force headquarters where intelligence officers jumped to the conclusion that the markers were the work of fifth columnists. The pictures were released by a major whose background included the stint as Hollywood and Broadway press agent, and caused a twenty-four hour sensation!

I mention this last example because of the hair-trigger, nuclear-neurosis situation in which we now live and the much greater possibili-ties of real public panic that may be created by managed news or promo-tional news. Similarly, if the public is conditioned to take its cue from government, it is apt at times to be misled as it was in the immediate hours after the U-2 incident. For instance, in the U-2 aftermath, the believing *New York Times* actually chided the Soviets for being so alarmed about "an accidental violation of Russian air rights." As creator of the initial impact through newspapers, the government occupies a privileged position in opinion-making and can only be checked for error or for evil by a vigorous press which has access to the same information in order to provide context, counterpoint, and if necessary, contradiction for government communiques. A one-way relationship ultimately breeds either submissiveness or suspicion.

The classic case of the clash between the press and genuine national security occurred in 1942 when in June the *Chicago Tribune* and other papers printed a dispatch written by a reporter who had spent time with our Pacific fleet, a dispatch headed: "U.S. Navy knew in advance all about Jap fleets." Infuriated government officials called for an investiga-tion, fearing the article had tipped off the Japanese that the U.S. Navy had access to special sources of information and, therefore, might dry up those sources. Attorney General Francis Biddle announced a Grand Jury investigation. The *Tribune* greeted the charges as ridiculous, claimed the investigation was inspired by Secretary of the Navy Knox, former publisher of the rival *Chicago Daily News,* invoked Jefferson's maxim, "Our liberty depends on the freedom of the press and can't be limited without being lost," and said the reporter had gotten his information from open-source material anyway. Later the Grand Jury decided "that no indictment should be returned . . . and that no violation of the law was disclosed . . ." Meanwhile other elements of the American press hinted at what these special sources of information on the Japanese fleet might be, and the key words code and cipher appeared extensively in the American press as it commented on the tussle between the *Tribune* and the government. Significantly, and luckily, the Japanese either did not notice or did not believe the possibility that their code had been broken, a most grave development for them. Of course, the code had been broken and played a part in this specific sea battle and others that followed.

Are there such genuine threats to national security today because of the press?

Roger Tubby, veteran press secretary of the Truman era and now in a similar key role with the State Department, has written me that:

There have been numerous stories, particularly regarding weapons and military operations under consideration which have appeared from time to time which, it seems to me, may have been of benefit to our potential enemies. Some of the stories have come from manufacturers who like to boast of their new products, some from officers who are proud of what their respective services are doing. Some are the result of probing by reporters.

Trade journals are often a major source of breaches of security concerning technology, weapon design, etc. Mr. Tubby did not mention another source: the deliberate leak by trial-ballooners or by the disgruntled, status-seeking middle-bureaucrats.

Veteran newsmen, however, do not fear such breaches as Tubby does, but question, in retrospect, whether or not a showing of real damage to national security can be made even when specific breaches are admitted.

It is not as easy as one might think to make a showing of damage to our national security as a result of the freedom of the press. We cannot demonstrate that which is unknowable. Neither can we always point with certainty to damage done to our freedoms each time national security momentarily impinges on the freedom of the press. The atom bomb was built behind a veil of secrecy which shielded even the man who later ordered its use, and the wartime restrictions on the press during World War II were dissolved without great difficulty.

Yet the new forms of repression — delay, distortion, managing and withholding the news by the government — may actually be more of a threat to national security than a free press, even if one considers *only* the military point of view. Instead of being assuaged administratively, our nation, for instance, would have been better off to have learned emphatically long before Lebanon, Laos, and Berlin that we were woefully weak in airlift capacity and in modern conventional weapons. A previously informed and attentive public may have responded so as to have made it unnecessary for a new president to contemplate the sickening prospect of simultaneous military involvement in Laos, Berlin, and Cuba with armed forces actually equipped to deal conventionally with only the nearest of these problems. A wider range of Executive choices can often be provided if the public is informed and supportive. This, I submit, is good for military strategy and good for national security. To feed the public placebo merely to avoid temporary turbulence may only create chaos later.

Should there be added access by the press to the *sanctum sanctorum* where the big decisions are made?

President Eisenhower took the position that:

Just as no private citizen or business entity can conduct its business under constant public scrutiny, so judges, legislators, or executive officials cannot conduct all public business at every step of the way in public.

Eisenhower argued that the question —

is not one of nondisclosure as to what was done, but rather whether the preliminary developmental processes of arriving at a final judgment need to be subjected to publicity. Obviously, they cannot be if government is to function.

Kennedy said at his first press conference that ". . . I do not hold the view that all matters and all information which is available to the Executive should be made available at all times . . ."

Jenkin Lloyd Jones, formerly president of the American Society of Newspaper Editors, said, "For it is only behind closed doors . . . that most politicians — yea, even statesmen — honestly express their views and try to get at the meat of the question." It is my own opinion that sometimes officials often seek shelter in secrecy not because they wish to hide *per se,* but because of the sometimes inevitable clash of political pride with the need for honest and practical performance. The glare of publicity sometimes mitigates against candor, change and concession — necessary ingredients of decision-making — and officials fear the public will not listen long enough or sincerely enough to understand or fully appreciate their actions. This is the cross the Capital *cognoscenti* see themselves as having to bear occasionally. In addition, many officials have, at times, been stung by the irresponsible actions of a newsman who was careless with a quote or who had his headline in mind before an interview. Though such actions are not typical, some doors are closed to the fourth estate by its own actions.

The serious difficulties a closed *sanctum sanctorum* presents for a democracy can be illustrated by the 1954 public statements made by high Department of Defense officials indicating that Russian capabilities in the long-range bomber and missile field were far less than they were later proven to be. The public, the Congress, and many policy-making officials were seriously misled. At this same time classified intelligence estimates were actually available which gave a far more realistic, and, as it later developed, accurate view of Russian air strength.

In my opinion, the public deserves much more of the decisive dialogue — the running record of the reasons for and against alternative courses of action — not just to be told in the press or otherwise of decisions. This does not mean allowing the public or press to watch a president make up his mind, but allowing us to know what things proved persuasive or placental, and what risks remain. Usually, the public gets much of the dialogue, anyway, but only in fragmented form and after delay; and a public possessed of partial truth may be "a prelude to a farce or a tragedy."

Although the Constitutional Convention was closed, the opinion-makers later engaged in a full-scale debate and discussion in speech and press before the recommendations of that body were finally affirmed, and the Federalist papers reproduced many of the arguments of Convention Hall and provided insight into the "whys" and the alternative considerations available in that great decision affecting national security.

This goal of an increase in the openness of the dialogue of our democracy's decision-makers will require a greater access by the press and public to the goings on of the Executive Branch than exists today — or has for some time, because that branch has acquired both the major ingredients of power: dollars and data. It has also acquired the built-in bias of all bureaucracies: not what *must* we *keep* from the public, but what *must* we *tell* them!

We cannot live openly as a society and hope to have many secrets. Even a few selected secrets will constitute a challenge to the press and test the discretion of the secret-bearers in a lubricated, cocktail society. If we wish to change the kind of society in which we live, let us change it directly, and not indirectly. If we wish to be open and free, then we must learn to say stoutly with Popeye, "I yam what I yam," and prepare ourselves to accept the risks and frustrations of freedom.

The ultimate decision in this whole struggle rests with the people. Justice Sutherland once observed that "a free press stands as one of the great interpreters between the government and the people. To allow it to be fettered is to fetter ourselves."

We must face, however, the fact that many people do not object to being fettered — if they are trustingly tethered to a fulsome federal trough! We must face the possibility that Eric Sevareid may be right: the complexity of our time may have outrun our comprehension and, therefore, we may finally resort to "one human being of commanding quality to make it all work out and to lead us."

However, if we do not regard our citizen-system as impotent, collision of opinion is still vital, and it cannot occur without a free press which has enough information of integrity. This condition affects our practical here-and-now political processes, as well as philosophical principles. The last election might well have ended differently if the press and public had been in a position during the 1960 elections to evaluate the missile gap which became a missile-lead. Note, too, how recently it has been our communication media, not primarily our government, that have provided us with various and dissenting views in civil defense which have probed into the most horrendous aspects of this problem. All of this democratic dialogue may lead us into a more meaningful program with greater public support than that originally announced, fiat-like, in the fall of 1961 by the Kennedy administration.

We must not make the mistake either, however, of relying on public opinion of the Greek City-democracy variety for *constant* and *meaningful* involvement in public affairs. Excesses and crises are often necessary to sharpen large-scale public opinion in a large, compartmentalized democracy. We must realize also that there may not be adequate time to bring a quick-breaking issue into full focus even if all the facts are known.

A few will or must decide for us all at times. But the elected decision-makers themselves will very frequently be fresh from our own midst, and this is another reason for a pervasive press that proceeds freely as if all citizens read and care. Another reason is that the decision-makers usually move and live among an attentive elite who can hopefully provide an arena — however small — where collision instead of collusion can then occur, because most executives sooner or later, in the interests of harmony and respite, act to insure that only like-minded colleagues cluster close to the throne.

Total national security, therefore, cannot exist without a free press — whether to service only the attentive or all — a free press which can help to call the cultural cadence, which prods us when we become lethargic as individuals, and which warns us of dangers when our sentinels sleep or are strangely silent. Information is our political plasma, our lifeblood, and it is better to risk an occasional hemorrhage affecting national security than to risk sluggishness and finally stoppage in the flow of fact: a hemorrhage may be inconvenient; yet it may constitute a kind of political shedding of "blood" which reveals national sin and without which there can be no repentance or remission.

Comments

HAYS GOREY

Mr. Maxwell predicted in a note to me several days ago that he would be shot down in flames as a result of the speech he has delivered tonight.

May I be the first to announce the dissolution of any antiaircraft — or anti-Maxwell — batteries I may have been able to muster. Rather than shoot Mr. Maxwell down, I prefer to keep him flying — as one of the most eloquent and articulate defenders of the free press outside the profession itself.

Such defenders — as I am sure Mr. Smart will agree — are not easy to come by any more, if indeed they ever were.

The question: "Is Freedom of the Press Compatible With National Security" demands at the outset certain concessions from those of us who would answer yes.

First — would a government unfettered by a probing, pesky press be able to move, act and even achieve much — and in less time? Of course.

Second — is a government impeded, delayed or even on occasion wrongfully dissuaded from a proper course of action by a free press, or the fact of a free press? Certainly.

Third — is there risk of ill-timed, erroneous and even injurious disclosures in a free press society? There is.

But large as these risks have loomed in the past, and as large as they loom for the future, they are dwarfed by the alternative.

Why? Because the alternative — an America without a free press — would not be America at all.

It may logically be argued that an America laid waste because of disclosures in its free press would not be America, either. Very true. But in an age fraught with perils, we have neither time nor resources to combat long-shots. And I submit that the risk of *lasting* damage to the national security, through an act of folly or irresponsibility by a free press, is indeed a long-shot.

Chancellor Kerr of the University of California said recently: "The open market-place is the only atmosphere in which democratic principles can be expected to survive." Without a press that is free, there is no open market-place — for ideas, for analysis, for criticism. If we are willing to torpedo any one of our basic freedoms in the name of national security, *then we are sinking the ship we profess to be saving.*

In the first place, America's strength does not rest on weaponry alone. Its security is not completely wrapped up in the number of missiles it has ready for launching. It rests also upon men and women, and such intangibles as ideas and energy. I think most of us here tonight will agree that the United States is stronger, not weaker, because it is an open society. We are encircled by known perils — but we are not quaking before *unknown* perils, thanks to free press and free speech. The Soviet citizen — who was not even aware when his government resumed nuclear testing — cannot say as much.

Times change, as Mr. Maxwell has pointed out. What was suitable to the simplicity of our colonial society may indeed be unsuitable — even a danger — in the nuclear age.

But we have not yet reached the stage where we need to pattern ourselves after, or borrow anything from, a monolithic society. And if we sacrifice a basic freedom on the altar of proclaimed national security, that is precisely what we will be doing.

Mr. Maxwell recognizes all this. But what he fears is the smothering effect of a goliath-like government on the press's ability — not to remain free in name — but in actuality.

There is cause for such concern.

As Oscar and Mary Handlin have written: "It may well be that our time will best be remembered for its painful and tenuous, yet immensely exhilarating, effort to allow men to be free."

And so it will be in the battle to maintain press freedom. There *will* be a battle. There always has been, because although God made no man wise enough to be a censor, he created millions who regard themselves as wise enough. Now lest the wrong impression be afoot, there will be no battle by the press for the right to "tip" an enemy to a military deployment; there will be no demand for access to the secret formula for creating a neutron bomb; an enterprising reporter will curb his enterprise short of revealing the whereabouts of a Polaris-armed submarine — unless, of course, the Russians already know.

It will battle to learn why — if the Titan missile blows up in six out of seven tests — such a shoddy record came about and why it is tolerated. (The Soviet press would not.) It will battle to learn why the Cuban fiasco was a fiasco, and who was to blame, and to insure that it will not happen again. (The Soviet press has not been reported delving into the reasons for the wall in Berlin, the background of the Hungarian rebellion, or the defection of Albania.)

Does not Cuba offer a prime example of press freedom and national security? Are we stronger — or weaker — because our involvement was so thoroughly aired, because our mistakes were pinned down? Are we stronger or weaker because — while we may well make mistakes in a similar situation in the future — we won't make the same mistakes? For its immediate effect, the full airing of the Cuban disaster perhaps did injure the United States. Its long-range effect can only be a strengthening of our national security.

At this point, it is necessary to interject that the free press will not conduct its battle free of error, any more than it has been free of error in the past. Democracy — and any facet of it — implies some trial and some error. But the end result, despite some stumbling along the way, will be a stronger society because it can withstand openness, because it would rather risk a leaky faucet than throw out the entire plumbing system.

As to Mr. Maxwell's concern over the power to panic, it perhaps exists. But so does the more frequently exercised power to prevent panic — through knowledge broadly disseminated. The rural groundmarking incident — with all the trappings of Hollywood press agentry — created a sensation, but not a panic. And when it was all over, the American citizen knew the explanation was one honestly arrived at — and not decreed by government edict.

There is more to fear in the unknown than there is in the known, and therefore our society, or any society whose press is free, is less likely to panic than one which gropes in the dark. It is also less likely to be fooled.

Mr. Maxwell suggests a possible false report of some sort which could send a nation with nuclear neurosis into basement shelters — prematurely. I should like to crawl out on a limb right now and say categorically that an unverified report of such magnitude would not find its way into the free press of the United States.

As to the U-2 incident, Mr. Maxwell rightly chides the press for gullibly swallowing the government's original explanation. He describes the government as "the creator of the original impact" through newspapers. In the U-2 case, it was. But no one need be misled by one spectacular failure into believing that the government has complete control of this original impact, or that it ever will have.

As many a bumbling bureaucrat has learned, as many a militarist, president, senator, businessman, and labor leader has learned, a free press can be fooled for a time. It can be unwittingly manipulated for a time. But it will not abrogate the right it has reserved to itself, and with which it has been entrusted, for very long. If it ever does, then of course there is no longer a free press.

Predictably, perhaps, I have discounted the real damage to national security from breaches of secrecy. Actual damage, as Mr. Maxwell has said, is unknowable. And that is why there is no cut and dried answer to the question at hand.

Certainly, there can be no underestimating the difficulties ahead in maintaining a press that is free. The day we live in is more complex. The issues are more numerous. There are more persons engaged in concealing them.

But journalists, too, are more numerous, and more skillful. They are, in large part, specialists who understand their subjects and who — more important — understand how to ferret out facts. And they are bolstered by the tradition that truth will out.

National security — national strength — is increased, not threatened, by a free press. The Handlins have described our way of living as "the way of a people who wished so to order their institutions that they would be able themselves to make the decisions important to them."

Without a press that is free, they would be unable to do so. And thus the question: "Is Freedom of the Press Compatible With National Security?" suggests another: "Can a government be truly and lastingly strong — and I stress the word lastingly — if its people are not strong enough to face — and discuss — the truth?"

Despite the presently awesome strength of Soviet Russia, I am convinced that it cannot.

WILLIAM B. SMART

I want first to express my respect for Neal Maxwell. He has enjoyed significant experiences and has made fine contributions in government, in university affairs, and in public life. His present paper is the result of careful scholarship, which I also respect. With all this experience and study, it is refreshing to note that Mr. Maxwell has arrived at precisely the same conclusions that many of us in journalism have long since reached.

I am also happy to associate myself with Mr. Gorey's thoughtful comments, and particularly acknowledge, with him, the shortcomings of America's press, along with its accomplishments.

Without belaboring the points Mr. Gorey has made so well, I would like to take quick issue with just one point in Mr. Maxwell's treatise. That is his fear of panic on the part of the people if certain sensitive information is made public. The record, in both peace and war, simply does not justify that fear. My experience is that the people of this country are far more tough-minded and can take far more than their would-be protectors would have us believe. We have not come close to fathoming the strength of character of our people.

Two or three other points in Mr. Maxwell's discussion might bear further emphasis and illustration, in passing.

Josephus Daniels was eminently correct when he said that "God never made a man wise enough to be a censor." But we are foolish enough to try. An acquaintance received a letter from a correspondent in the Pacific Theater during World War II, in which the censors had left little more than the greeting and the signature. But somehow a copy of the same letter, sent to another man, had slipped through unscathed. After the war, when the two copies were compared, it developed that the censored material dealt not with troop movements or other classified matter, but almost entirely with the stupidity of army censors.

Second, I liked particularly Mr. Maxwell's insistence that just announcing decisions to the public is not enough; we must also know the reasons and the arguments and the compromises that went into making those decisions. There is a considerable body of thought to the contrary. One of the leaders of such thought on one occasion wrote:

Our law concerning the press is such that divergencies of opinion between members of the government are no longer an occasion for public exhibitions, which are none of the newspapers' business. We've eliminated that conception of political freedom which holds that everybody has the right to say whatever comes into his head.

The author of that bit of political philosophy was Adolf Hitler, and his statement reveals one of the foundation stones upon which he built his evil structure.

Perhaps the most impressive argument for Mr. Maxwell's position defending freedom of the press as compatible with national security is the history of the most recent attempt to challenge it. The memory is still fresh.

President Kennedy, stung and shook up by the Cuban invasion fiasco last April (1961), went before the American Association of Newspaper Editors and implied that newspapers were homehow responsible for the mess we were in, and suggested that the profession set up a system of voluntary self-censorship to avoid damaging the nation's security. The editors took up the challenge immediately. Leaders of representative press groups met with the President, offered their co-operation, and asked for his suggestions. After eighty minutes of discussion, the editors came away without any specific suggestions as to how they could better meet their responsibilities to the national security. There was a half-hearted announcement that another meeting would be held "some months later," but to date no such meeting has been held or scheduled. In other words, the project has been quietly dropped, and the inference must be that it was dropped because more careful study showed no real problem exists.

Now, briefly and specifically, my own position is this:

1. The newspapers of America have done a remarkably responsible job of protecting the national security where actual sensitive information is involved. The history of the press both in wartime and in what now passes for peace is a proud one in this respect.

2. In a day of concern over decreasing numbers of newspapers and more and more concentration of power in the hands of a few, it is at least encouraging that the more responsible papers are the ones that are surviving while the shallow, sensational newspapers are the ones going to the wall. For example, note that Hearst papers have failed in recent years in Oakland, San Francisco, Chicago, and, just this week, Los Angeles.

3. Conflict between government and newspapers, in Washington as well as in City Hall, arises not so much over issues of real national security as over issues of bureaucratic security that is, where information is withheld to shield officials or employees from charges of bungling, or worse.

4. I believe in the people of America. I believe that however dangerous the times in which we live, we need not fear decisions made by an intelligently informed public.

At least two previous speakers in this Great Issues series have declared that the greatest danger to this nation, over the long, difficult period of which President Kennedy speaks, is that in fighting a ruthless enemy we will adopt his methods. I believe this to be true. That danger is equally present in the conflict of free access of the press to government information versus the power of, and ever-present tendency toward, censorship.

Indeed, if there is a legitimate fear for national security in relation to the press, it is that pressures against free disclosure of information might create a society in which the public no longer demands or is given the information vital to the effective working of democracy.

There was a great man who died under tragic circumstances not long ago, a real hero in the fight for peace. Shortly before his death, when he was waging a heroic fight for peace, he had some words to say on tonight's subject of discussion. The man I speak of is Dag Hammarskjold, late secretary general of the United Nations. During his fight to retain the integrity of his office against those who would destroy it, he had this to say to the Security Council:

It is futile to argue with those to whom truth is a function of party convenience, and justice a function of party interests. But for others, it may be essential that some facts be recalled and simply put on the record.

Where, then, lies America's national security? This nation can remain free and secure only as long as truth does not become a function of party — or bureaucratic — convenience; only as long as the American public continues to insist that facts be recalled and clearly put on the record.

4

What Are the Relations Between Freedom and the National Economy?

JEWELL J. RASMUSSEN

Perhaps at no other time in the history of the United States has the issue of economic freedom been more important than it is today. It is doubtful that there has ever been another era with as many groups and associations — from the John Birch Society on the extreme right to the Communist associations on the extreme left — whose programs are directly concerned with the economic freedom of the American people. It is quite likely that the list of special problems involving moral and social responsibility in economic affairs is longer today than at any other time in our history. On this list would be found such matters as these:

1. The growing power of the large corporations.
2. Diminishing effective competition.
3. Price fixing by business firms (e.g., the recent electrical-equipment industry and the Utah Pharmaceutical Association).
4. Personal ethics of businessmen.
5. Strong-arm tactics and gangsterism in some labor unions.
6. Taste and truth in advertising.
7. Deceptive packaging and labeling of products.
8. Economic insecurity for various groups of persons.
9. Instability in the economy.
10. Economically depressed areas.
11. The farm problem.
12. Chronic unemployment.
13. Inadequacy of some public services.
14. Economic aid to underdeveloped countries.

All of these matters, and many more related ones, affect directly or indirectly the degree of economic freedom enjoyed by the American people. The growing complexity of our economy and the seriousness of some of the matters named above require corrective actions by the people through their local, state, and federal governments that often reduce to some extent our personal and private economic freedom in order that the community and national welfare may be increased.

But herein lies the crux of our problem. The ultraconservatives take the position that government has already encroached entirely too far in our economic affairs and should retreat extensively from present activities. The conservatives regard many types of present-day governmental activities as "creeping socialism." As a major spokesman for the conservative viewpoint in the West, Ezra Taft Benson, for example, has stated this position as follows:

It is my conviction that the paramount issue today is liberty against creeping socialism. Collectivized socialism is part of the Communist strategy. Communist dupes and leftwingers use every strategum to make socialism sound appealing and seem inevitable. Their aims for the U.S. include greatly expanded wasteful spending, higher and higher taxes, increasingly unbalanced budgets, wild inflation followed by government controls, greater centralization of power in Washington, and so on ad infinitum.[1]

For thirty years we have aided the cause of atheistic, socialistic communism by ... squandering much of our material resources; by recklessly spending ourselves to near bankruptcy; by weakening our free enterprise system through adoption of socialistic policies; by wasteful bungling of our foreign affairs; by ever increasing confiscatory taxation....

When socialism is understood, we will realize that many of the programs advocated, and some of those already adopted in the U.S. fall clearly within the category of socialism.[2]

No true ... American can be a socialist or a communist or support programs leading in that direction.[3]

On the other hand there are groups of individuals who strongly believe that the U.S. economy is lagging far behind its potential and urge greater governmental effort and spending to stimulate the economy to a better level of performance. Typical of such groups is the following statement:

Neither the Sputnik nor the Lunic nor the Russian spacetraveler, neither the events in Cuba nor Laos nor elsewhere, and neither the fourth economic recession since World War II nor the chronic ailment of an economic growth rate only one-third to one-half that of some industrialized countries both free and hostile, have yet aroused the United States to action suited to the times.

To be sure, the President and others have spoken eloquently in general terms about the challenge and the need to meet it. And the President's specific economic program, so far as it goes, deserves for the most part unalloyed support. But there is a growing consensus that, in economic matters as in others, we continue at our peril to underestimate the difficulties confronting us and the massive exertions required to surmount them.

---

[1] *Deseret News and Salt Lake Telegram,* Church News Section, September 2, 1961, p. 14.

[2] *Ibid.,* December 23, 1961, p. 15.

[3] *Improvement Era* (December, 1961), p. 955.

This frustration on the economic front, which underpins all other fronts, is not due to insuperable political difficulties, nor to any intrinsic weakness among the American people. It is not due to lack of the economic knowledge and tools which could lift performance to the level of our unrivaled potentials and imperative needs. It is due rather to continuing commitment, in many high places, to the delusion that something will turn up without very much new and redirected effort, accompanied by reluctance to initiate programs which break drastically with traditions suitable in easier times.

The frail and inconclusive economic upturn now in process cannot override the fact that the American economy is afflicted with the chronic ailment of low economic growth, made manifest in a consistent "roller-coaster" pattern of successive "booms," "stagnations," and "recessions." This chronic ailment has worsened in the long-run.[4]

Thus the issue is drawn between the conservatives who desire to increase the economic freedom of individuals by substantially reducing public services and the liberals who would prefer to sacrifice some individual freedom, if necessary, in order to secure a more satisfactory performance of the economy.

With respect to this issue of economic freedom, the conservatives often expressly state or imply that any departure from "rugged individualism" is un-American, that this type of economic system should not be tampered with or changed in any way. Let me remind you, in the words of Ben W. Lewis of Oberlin College, just what an economic system is.

. . . an economic system, a political economy, is a set of man-made and man-accepted arrangements designed to economize our natural and human resources; that is, to bring about the constant and continuing use of these resources as men, in society, want them to be used. . . . We are forced by the basic conditions of our life together to economize our resources and, thus, to establish and everlastingly to re-establish arrangements suited to the performance of the economizing task as we want it performed.

The economic system in operation in any country at any time represents the way in which the people of that country, at that time and as they are then persuaded, want the economizing function in their society to be performed. In our own case, we place heavy reliance upon the forces of (1) free, individual initiative and choice, (2) economic (profit) motivation, and (3) unrestrained rivalry (competition) between independent, profit-seeking sellers and between independent, profit-seeking or satisfaction-seeking buyers.[5]

No economic system, however, is likely to be "pure" — whether it be "market" or "Marxist." Our own economy is not entirely a "market" economy but rather is a "mixed" one. Lewis has described it well in these words:

[4] Conference on Economic Progress, *Jobs and Growth* (May 1961), p. 1.

[5] Ben W. Lewis, "Economics by Admonition," *American Economic Review, Papers and Proceedings* (May 1959), pp. 385–86.

Competitive profit-seeking in the free market is the core of our economizing process, but we have never been satisfied and happy with the core alone. All economic systems are made from day to day, they undergo constant modification and revision to accomplish the economic purposes which men, in their own time and their own environment, deem to be good. The machinery for establishing and changing the formal structure of the economy is political, and it is invoked whenever enough people are moved to call it into operation on specific issues. Whenever enough of us become dissatisfied with the structure or processes of the economy as it exists or displeased with the results which it produces, we exercise our collective political will: we "economize" consciously by government. . . . Through government we supplement the market; we also supplant the market. Our total, over-all economy, thus, is a complex and constantly changing mixture of profit-seeking, competitively-controlled individualism, and conscious, governmentally organized and operated collectivism, built up piece by piece, to serve the desires of our politically free people as they express their desires in political economic decisions.[6]

In the process of supplementing the market mechanism, it is important that such modifying actions be made in a thoroughly democratic manner by majority vote and not by minority pressure-group tactics.

In the remainder of this paper, three basic areas will be explored in which the American people have supplemented the profit-seeking market system or in which further governmental action might be undertaken: (1) regulation or protection of the public, (2) economic assistance to particular groups in the economy, and (3) controlling instability and promoting full employment. A fourth area, our national goals and foreign economic policy, is touched upon briefly.

Regulation or Protection of the Public

To the conservative, the lengthening list of regulatory agencies at both the state and federal levels of government and the growing number of restrictive laws affecting business in particular are sure signs that socialism is just around the corner unless these trends can be reversed. To the liberal, on the other hand, the growing power of the big corporations, quiz-show rigging, conflict of interest scandals, price collusion, the Tower of Babel situation existing in advertising and selling practices, all indicate that more and tougher restrictions must be imposed on business.

The regulation of business activities is regarded by some people as being of fairly recent origin; however, this is not the case. We can go back to the towns in Europe in the twelfth century, for example, and find a most elaborate regulatory system. In these towns control was

---

[6] *Ibid.*, p. 387.

first exercised by the merchant guilds and then later to an increasing extent by the craft guilds. These guilds, including both masters and artisans, undertook the regulations of all the industrial processes in each town. Elaborate codes were developed by which prices and conditions of sale were fixed, wages regulated, hours and working relations determined, and workmanship and product quality attested. These guilds became rather general governing bodies, setting up customs barriers against other towns and rural districts, and controlling many matters both directly and indirectly connected with the interests of the townspeople. This tight control system was mainly a local system.

In the latter part of the Middle Ages, localism gave way to nationalism, or the national point of view, called "mercantilism." Mercantilism was also characterized by regulation — regulation aimed at making a state strong by economic means. Controls were directed toward an increasing population, low wages and cheap food, cheap raw materials, priority to foreign trade with a favorable balance of trade to cause an inward flow of gold and silver, stimulating export trade by bounties, tax exemption, trade treaties, etc. Commercial and manufacturing preponderance was the goal sought and all political and financial resources were marshaled toward this end. Interference with private enterprise was considered fully justified if prompted by state policy aimed at the promotion of well being of the state. Mercantilism prevailed generally among European statesmen from the sixteenth to the latter part of the eighteenth century.

During the first century of our national history, public policy became inextricably intertwined with the process of exploitation and development of a virgin land. Economic and legal institutions were shaped to facilitate this expansion. The government itself played a vigorous role in promoting economic development and in establishing the foundations for the growth of business enterprise.

Likewise, it should be noted that as the century advanced, one sector after another came under corporate sway. With the gradual relaxation on corporate size and activity came growing political power of corporate promoters. With increases in the size of individual business firms also came increasing power on the part of businessmen to shape and control the national economy. Thus, although the first century of our history saw the gradual triumph of laissez-faire doctrine, the stage was set for the return of government regulation.

The beginnings of the regulatory movement in the United States are usually associated with the Granger activities of the 1870's. Some efforts were made before this time, of course, but, following the agrarian tradition of Jefferson and Jackson, these early efforts were largely expressed through local and state governments, thus delaying national regulation of economic life for some years.

Although the Granger movement was to a large extent associated with the initiation of effective railroad regulation, it also had a wider program; it was antimoney power, antimonopoly, and antimiddleman. The agitation begun by the Granger movement eventually resulted in the creation of the Interstate Commerce Commission in 1887, and thus a foundation was laid for national assumption of regulation in the field of economic enterprise.

In contrast to the views of many conservatives, the situation inaugurating national regulation of the railroads has been the pattern for most of the other national regulations since 1887. The following statement by Fainsod and Gordon emphasizes this point:

> The more one ponders the history of the growth of regulation in the United States, the clearer it becomes also that this growth has not been the product of any farsighted plan or design or the result of any thoroughly worked out rationale or theory. Step by step, whether in state or nation, it has represented a series of empirical adjustments to felt abuses. It has been initiated by particular groups to deal with specific evils as they arose, rather than inspired by any general philosophy of governmental control.[7]

In its modern aspects, the principal regulatory or protective problem is found in the economic power of giant corporations — and some labor unions. In contrast to the mid-nineteenth-century nation of farmers, shopkeepers, and small manufacturers, our economy today is dominated by a powerful corporate machine. In the modern corporation, the owner is, in general, a passive recipient, control is typically in the hands of management, and management usually selects its own replacements. To emphasize their power, A. A. Berle tells us: "Some of these corporations are units which can be thought of only in somewhat the way we have heretofore thought of nations."[8]

The concentration of economic activity in corporations in the United States is easily demonstrated. A few selected comparisons will confirm this point.

1. Of the 4.7 million business firms in the United States, less than 1 per cent account for nearly three-fifths (59 per cent) of all paid employment.

---

[7] Merle Fainsod and Lincoln Gordon, *Government and the American Economy* (New York: W. W. Norton, 1948), p. 226.

[8] A. A. Berle, Jr., *Economic Power and the Free Society* (New York, 1957), p. 15.

2. The 500 largest business corporations account for about two-thirds of all nonagricultural economic activity.

3. The 202 largest nonfinancial corporations have combined assets in excess of $165 billion.

4. The 44 largest firms with research and development laboratories, account for some 45 per cent of the total number of technicians and scientists and 50 per cent of research expenditures.

5. The 100 companies that received the largest defense contracts between July 1950 and June 1956 received nearly two-thirds of the value of all defense contracts during this period. The largest 10 contractors accounted for almost one-third of the total contracts.[9]

Concomitant with economic power is social and political power. Professor Chayes of Harvard Law School has stated well this point as follows:

Economic power is not the whole story, however, nor perhaps even its most important part. Concern with the modern corporation is intensified to the extent that its activities have necessarily ramified beyond the economic sphere of production of goods and service.

Across a widening range of activity, the large corporations have become principal factors. They are the chief agencies of private research. They are the hope of fund raisers for institutions of higher learning and the principal consumers of the products of those institutions. Their advertising supports newspapers and sponsors TV programs. They are a leading, if not the leading, purveyor of influence and pressure on public officials in Washington and state capitols.

It follows that in these spheres and others they bear large responsibility for the quality and tone of American life. The neglect of basic research, the dilution of the college degree, the organization man, the dullness and superficiality of the mass media, the level of political morality — all these offspring, wanted or unwanted, find their way in the end to the doorstep of the modern corporation.

This attribution of responsibility is not a token of hostility to the large private corporation. What has been said amounts to no more than that the great corporation is the dominant nongovernmental institution of modern American life. The university, the labor union, the church, the charitable foundation, the professional association — other potential institutional centers — are all, in comparison, both peripheral and derivative.[10]

Such is the position of the large corporation in the United States today. The critical question is, of course, whether society wants to try to limit or control the power of the large corporations and whether it can

---

[9] Carl Kaysen, "The Corporation: How Much Power? What Scope?" in Edward S. Mason, ed., *The Corporation in Modern Society* (Cambridge, Mass.: Harvard University Press, 1959), p. 86.

[10] Abram Chayes, "The Modern Corporation and the Rule of Law," *ibid.*, pp. 26–27.

be done. Three alternative possibilities appear to be available: (1) the limitation of corporate power by promoting more effective competition; (2) broader and more satisfactory control of business power by governmental agencies; and (3) the institutionalization within the firm and responsibility for the exercise of power.[11] All three are possibilities although the first is not very probable; and all will be difficult. Some form of federal control seems to be the most feasible or perhaps a combination of the second and third types of control.

The urgency of doing something along these lines is evident from the recent revelations of misdoings by business: quiz-show rigging, price collusion, stock market manipulations, bid rigging, misleading advertising, etc. The indictment of business for these malpractices has been made by business itself. The magazine *Sales Management* put the indictment as follows:

> The storm against business is blowing up big. Coast to coast, private citizens, public officials, the press and businessmen themselves are heard wondering about "What's happening to business?"
> Not in 50 years has a relatively normal, peacetime economy witnessed such a mountainous wave of sentiment against so many business practices. Some call it a breakdown in morals, some a lack of ethical standards. From every side come outright attacks, insinuations, dissatisfaction with the order of the "business house."
> Such attacks have a way of turning themselves into new laws, new Government orders, new "clean-ups" and "crackdowns" — all aimed at restricting the business world. It has happened more than once in the past and, unless business does something fast, it will happen again — soon.[12]

The article points out that the choice business must make is this: It can take matters in its own hands and close the social gap itself, or it can travel the road it has traveled so unsuccessfully many times before protesting loudly against unfair treatment and run the risk of having nothing to say about the restrictions that may be imposed. The article notes that the latter choice appears to be the one being made by many businessmen as they make speeches shifting the blame for offenses, trying to make sharp marketing practices look acceptable, raising the battle cry of "free enterprise," and so on. A partial answer to this attitude by the magazine article is put as follows:

> And the tired, old tale about every new restriction's spelling the absolute end of the American way of life has about run out of gas. Although this warning has been repeated over and over again, the number of citizens who feel

---

[11] Suggested by Carl Kaysen, *op. cit.*, p. 103.

[12] "The Business Inquisition," *Sales Management*, Part 1 of Two Parts (May 19, 1961), p. 35.

less free than they used to is definitely in the minority. Too often in the past business interests have equated liberty with unlimited self-gratification to leave much sting in this argument.[13]

In an open letter to top executives, the editors of *Sales Management* make this charge:

You have been challenged. As a corporate executive, as a business leader, you have been challenged by the inquisition to clean up your own house, or have it cleaned for you. . . .

The role of a corporate executive today is an important one in our economy. It is equally important in our society. And you cannot afford to forget that you are a part of that society — both as an individual and a businessman. You are indebted to it for your position and responsible to it for your actions. It is not an exaggeration to say that you are on a plane with members of Congress, governors of states, mayors of communities. The business you are entrusted to run must be operated in conformance with the rules, the tastes — and to some extent even the whims — of society, or society has the power and the right to revoke your franchise.[14]

I fully concur with this statement.

Although I agree with Professor Chayes of the Harvard Law School in the statement quoted previously that the giant corporation is the dominant nongovernmental institution of modern American life and that labor unions and other similar groups are both peripheral and derivative, I also believe that some labor unions are abusing their franchises, and it may be necessary for society to protect the public from such abuses of power and privilege. Unfortunately, some unions draw their leaders from a class which Professor Neil Chamberlain has characterized as adventurers. "Some of these adventurers may be pirates outside the law, carving out their own racket dominion within a gangster empire. Others may seek to stay this side of the law, or at least within some shady area where legal censure is uncertain."[15]

Congressional hearings in recent years have awakened public consciousness to the existence of this type of union leadership. "As one unsavory story followed another on the front pages of the daily newspapers, the association between unionism and corruption in our society seemed more and more confirmed — corruption in the forms of racketeering, gangsterism, and monopoly position secured by strong-arm methods."[16] Governmental action against such union practices seems to be a must.

---

[13] *Ibid.,* p. 39.

[14] *Ibid.,* p. 41.

[15] Neil Chamberlain, "The Corporation and the Trade Unions," in Mason, *op. cit.,* p. 128.

[16] *Ibid.*

In addition to these predatory activities of unions, the emergence of large unions covering whole industries has raised the question of "too much power" in the minds of many people. Likewise, the existence of small unions which possess great strategic power due to special skills or to a particular position in the market has long been a matter of public concern. An example of the latter is the recent slow-down at Cape Canaveral as a means of forcing overtime pay. Appropriate restrictive governmental action may be in order for both of these situations.

The special Committee for Economic Development's (CED) Labor Study Group has proposed a twofold approach to such use of private power. One is the use of checks and balances — strong employer associations to counteract union power — and the other is the limitation by government of the allowable uses of power without being subject to the antitrust laws.[17] The Labor Study Group also held that the recent disclosures of the abuse of union office, as well as other studies over longer periods of time, have clearly shown that public policy must play a part in assuring democratic procedures, minority rights, and financial integrity within unions.[18]

Economic Assistance to Particular Groups

Financial assistance and new programs or services for special groups by state or federal government are usually regarded by the conservatives as creeping socialism and hence are condemned. Such assistance programs or services originate for a variety of reasons: special interest groups, public policy to aid weak segments or groups in the economy, aspects of a program to reduce economic insecurity, and aspects of a general program to lessen somewhat the inequalities of wealth and income. There is much overlapping, obviously, among these casual forces and emphasis has varied considerably.

Most of the critics of these assistance programs fail to read American economic history, and hence they confine their criticism to the period of the 1930's and since. In so doing they overlook a most fundamental fact about government aid. It was business — not agriculture, not labor, not the aged, sick, unemployed, fatherless children — that first sought and received government assistance.

Alexander Hamilton was interested in the establishment of a strong central government drawing its principal support from the banking, commercial, and manufacturing industries and devoting its energies to

---

[17] "Collective Bargaining and the American Economy," *Saturday Review* (January 13, 1962), p. 34.

[18] *Ibid.,* p. 38.

promoting the growth of business enterprise in the United States. Thus the Hamiltonian program identified the prosperity of the nation with the prosperity of the business classes. The role of government in his system was to dispense privileges to business, and with business in a favored position, the resulting economic benefits would percolate to other groups and be diffused through the whole economy. This early assistance program has been well described as follows:

At the same time government played a vigorous role in promoting economic development and in establishing the foundations for the growth of business enterprise. The dearth of private capital for business enterprise made resort to public credit essential. Where prospective profits were too small to encourage private companies to undertake improvements, the state itself took the lead. Roads were built, bridges constructed, canals cut, and railroads laid by public authorities in order to advance the economic development of particular regions. Public resources were made freely available to private individuals. Loans were made to promote various projects for internal improvements, dams, turnpikes, canals, railroads, and even manufacturing enterprises. Government subscriptions to stock issues in connection with such enterprises were by no means uncommon. . . . Nor was state aid confined to assistance in the form of loans or stock subscriptions. Grants of land, lottery privileges, exemptions from taxation, and other devices were also employed as "encouragement" to private initiative.

Indeed, one of the dominating characteristics of the early history of government intervention in the United States is the extent to which public funds and public resources supported, stimulated, and promoted the spread of business enterprise. The exigencies of a young and undeveloped country carried the day for government aid.[19]

This early business promotionalism also inspired movements for agrarian and labor promotionalism and a competitive race for privileges was set in motion.

Over the years the federal government has acquired a wide variety of programs involving some element of subsidy, either direct or indirect. A mere listing of the major categories indicates the sweeping, amorphous character of these programs.

1. Grants to business firms and corporations to carry out specific objectives (shipbuilding differential).
2. Tax benefits to specific economic groups (depletion allowances to mineral producers).
3. Farm subsidy programs (commodity price support).
4. Indirect assistance to specific economic groups (protective tariffs).
5. Government economic programs with incidental economic effects similar to those of subsidies (stockpiling of strategic materials).

---

[19] Fainsod and Gordon, op. cit., pp. 223–224.

6. Free services or services below cost (statistical information to business and labor).
7. Lending and loan guarantee programs.
   A. Direct loans (low rent public housing).
   B. Loan guarantee and insurance (small business loans).
8. Insurance programs (veterans' life insurance).
9. Federal aid payments to states and local governments (hospital construction).
10. Federal aid payments to individuals (NSF research grants).[20]

Many of these subsidy programs have strong support from the public and serve broad public purposes but many also have come into existence solely by self-seeking pressure groups.

For those programs that are measurable, the net expenditures by major groups of beneficiaries were distributed as follows in three selected fiscal years.[21]

	(MILLIONS OF DOLLARS)		
	1951	1956	1960
Net current expenses for aids:			
Agriculture	905	1,846	3,568
Business	809	1,066	1,352
Labor	197	412	327
Homeowners and tenants	−160	−89	64
Additions to federal assets:			
Major commodity inventories — net change			
Civil ....−1,079		1,598	1,132
Major national security	769	451	192
Expenditures for other developmental purposes:			
Private assets	477	332	825
Total	1,918	5,616	7,460

As noted in this summary of direct, measurable subsidies, agriculture has received the largest share in most of the recent years. The continuation of these large subsidies year after year is not defensible. Time will

---

[20] Joint Economic Committee, U.S. Congress, *Subsidy and Subsidy-like Programs of the U.S. Government* (Washington, 1960), pp. 16–17.

[21] *Ibid.,* Table 1.

not permit an analysis of the whole complex farm problem, so I must be content with a few summary statements. From the economic point of view, the farm program of both Republican and Democratic administrations is not satisfactory. However, with the market structures we have in both the agricultural and business segments of our economy, it is unthinkable to pull the government completely out of agriculture. A program can be developed that will give us reasonable stability and better balance in agriculture and will also assure a growing nation of an adequate supply of food and fiber in the future. Such a program cannot be achieved without some help from the federal government, but it need not cost us as much as we are now paying.

To select another program for brief comment, the conservatives are highly critical of the social security program with the loss of personal freedom and responsibility resulting therefrom. Throughout the last twenty-five years, the program has developed and continually expanded under both Democratic and Republican administrations. In spite of the cries of socialism by some people, it is highly unlikely there will be any turning back from the course now being followed. The total program — old age annuities, aid to dependent children, unemployment compensation, etc. — serves two basic needs in the economy: it reduces economic insecurity in several important areas, and it adds considerably to the stability of the economy — both worthwhile objectives.

I am sure that some of you here tonight are familiar with Galbraith's book *The Affluent Society* and with his view that we must find a way to remedy the poverty which afflicts us in public services and which is in sharp contrast with our affluence in private goods. He argues that it is foolish to create demand for new goods by deliberately making existing consumer goods obsolete through style changes, for example, when there are so many ready-made needs for schools, hospitals, slum clearance, urban redevelopment, sanitation, and many other things of this type.[22]

To fill these needs requires tax dollars which deprive people of their freedom of choice in spending this portion of their income. My answer to this situation is full public debate on the relative merits of specific public needs versus the private uses of personal income. Then let the people decide at the ballot box. The inherent weakness of this method is the unevenness of the resources of the advocates and opponents of a given public program. Well-financed opponents can often unduly in-

---

[22] John Kenneth Galbraith, *The Affluent Society* (Boston: Houghton Mifflin Co., 1958), Chap. XXII.

fluence the issue by generous purchase of newspaper space and radio and television time.

A current example of the town-meeting approach is found in Ohio. Governor DiSalle and his aids are inaugurating a series of meetings in the large cities to present their case for more state support for four state programs — public schools, higher education, mental hygiene, and welfare. They hope to win public support through better understanding.

I was amazed to see the actual record of growth of new agencies and activities in Utah between 1945 and 1961. The August, 1959, issue of the Utah Foundation's "Research Report" listed some forty-five new programs that were begun — one of which has been discontinued. These additions include such major activities as two vocational schools, Utah Water and Power Board, the Legislative Council, checking stations, Tourist and Publicity Council, State Library Commission, Park and Recreation Commission, medical care for welfare cases, Coordinating Board for Higher Education, educational television, etc. The people in Utah apparently regard these public services as more important than the private goods and services foregone.

There is a great need, in my opinion, for careful and sincere discussion of programs calling for aid to particular groups or new programs in order that those public needs so vital and necessary to the functioning of a democracy and to the general well-being of the people will not be pushed aside or starved for funds by less important but high pressure programs. Perhaps no program has been debated more thoroughly over a longer period of time than federal aid to education. Here a program of broad general interest has been complicated by special issues of race and religion in addition to the central issues of fear of loss of state rights on the one hand and greater equality of opportunity and tax burden on the other hand.

Recent examples of programs calling for federal aid include such diverse activities as these: The president of the National Turkey Growers Association has stated that his association would ask for federal help in getting higher prices for turkeys as supply and demand produces a price too low for the growers. U.S. Secretary of Labor, Arthur J. Goldberg, has suggested that there be a government subsidy to the arts. President Kennedy has recommended the enactment of a health insurance program under the Social Security system for people who are sixty-five years old or older. Obviously these three proposals do not deserve equal consideration.

Controlling Instability and Promoting
a Full Employment Economy

There is a considerable amount of agreement among economists, based on substantial evidence, that there is a gulf between the feasible performance of the economy and its actual performance. There are quite a few people who believe that this gulf is likely to widen in the future. Although the general level of business activity has been fairly good since the end of World War II, the economy could clearly have performed more satisfactorily. Three areas of less than satisfactory behavior can be noted:

(1) Four economic contractions or recessions have occurred since 1947: 1948–49, 1953–54, 1957–58, and 1960–61. True, these have all been mild recessions — except for the millions who were unemployed. All four recessions have been reflected in sharp increases in unemployment, extending to all working groups. Furthermore, the level of unemployment remaining after each recession has been rising.

(2) Evidence is mounting that persistent unemployment may become a general, long-term problem. After the recession of 1947–49, unemployment fell to a level of about 3 per cent; after the 1953–54 recession, the ratio remained a little above 4 per cent; following the business decline of 1957–58, unemployment remained above 5 per cent; and now it is above 6 per cent. As the National Association of Manufacturers has stated:

> It would be a mistake to regard the economic difficulties with which the nation is presently (early 1961) confronted as merely a phase of the business cycle. We may indeed emerge rather quickly from the current recession. . . . But the economic record of recent years gives no ground for assurance that we will then automatically be back on the track of economic growth and full realization of the nation's productive potential.[23]

Hence, the problem of unemployment is a growing rather than a receding one. Unless there is a higher rate of growth of demand than in recent years with a steadily expanding labor market, it will be impossible to absorb workers displaced by machines and technological progress in general as well as the new workers added to the labor force each year.

The economy has slowed down in recent years as evidenced by such facts as these:[24]

---

[23] *Unemployment, Causes and Cures*, Economic Series No. 83 (New York, April 1961).

[24] *Staff Report on Employment, Growth, and Price Levels*, Joint Economic Committee, U.S. Congress (December 24, 1959), p. 67.

(a) The growth of real gross national product has decreased since 1953.

(b) As noted above, unemployment rates are higher in recent years than in the early postwar years.

(c) Productive capacity has been increasingly underutilized.

(d) The rate of increase of productivity has slowed.

(3) Throughout the nation, including Utah, there are depressed areas officially designated by the U.S. Labor Department as "chronic labor surplus areas," or more recently, "redevelopment areas." Utah has eight such areas at this time. These depressed areas, as a group, fare worse than the nation as a whole in a recession, and they usually do not experience the same degree of improvement as the country as a whole in the recovery period. Whereas the nation may have an unemployment ratio of 5 or 6 per cent, these depressed areas may have ratios of 10 to 15 per cent. There are some 45 or 46 major labor market areas and 140 to 145 smaller centers classified officially as "areas of substantial labor surplus."

The possibility of a serious unemployment problem following World War II was anticipated by passage of the Employment Act of 1946. This Act declared it to be ". . . the continuing policy and responsibility of the Federal Government to use all practicable means . . . to promote maximum employment, production, and purchasing power. . . ." While this is a good statement of intent, it has to be implemented by specific policies and actions.

There are policies and actions that can be taken to remedy or alleviate the various unemployment problems which I have briefly described. The important question is whether or not the federal government, with the assistance and co-operation of state and local governments, business, and labor, will inaugurate the appropriate policies and take the necessary actions to remedy the various unemployment problems. There are no easy or painless solutions — but there are solutions if we are willing to do what has to be done.

The most important policy for remedying unemployment in excess of the frictional minimum (say 4 per cent) is the maintenance of adequate effective demand for the goods and services of the economy. Supplementary measures are required to accelerate the recovery of areas affected by structural unemployment, and to reduce the frictional unemployment. There are appropriate measures for abating the severity and frequency of recessions, and for insuring adequate economic growth. Specific programs can be undertaken to improve the situation in chronically depressed areas. Measures are also needed to raise the

employability and economic status of certain disadvantaged groups in
the population. Policies to insure national prosperity will help, but will
certainly not eliminate, human distress resulting from changes in technology and the patterns of demand. The burden of such changes must
be equitably distributed.

On this broad question of jobs, technology, and the role of government, the January bulletin of the Center for the Study of Democratic
Institutions, an institution of the Fund for the Republic, has this to say
under the general theme "Caught on the Horn of Plenty":

The United States is advancing rapidly into a national economy in which
there will not be enough jobs of the conventional kind to go around. The
acceleration of technology is responsible. A social and political crisis will be
the result. Substitutes for such presently accepted goals as full employment
will have to be found. Fresh definitions of the conceptions of work, leisure,
abundance, and scarcity are needed. Economic theories adequate to an industrial revolution are not good enough for the conditions of the scientific revolution. The complexity and interdependence of the scientific-industrial state
calls for national planning. The individualism of the eighteenth and nineteenth centuries is a casualty of technology, as are old theories of private property. Government must intervene more and more in the nation's industrial
life. The destiny is the economy under law. A radical change in public
attitude toward law and government is necessary if the general welfare is to
be achieved. Having bargained for the benefits of technology on all fronts,
law is our only means of assuring that it serves the common good.

National Goals and Foreign Economic Policies

No discussion of this topic of freedom and the national economy
would be complete without some consideration of our national goals in
relation to our foreign economic policies. However, time will not permit
nor is the speaker qualified to delve into this aspect of the problem.
Hence, only a few summary statements will be made.

Our national goals in the field of foreign economic policy must be
related, of course, to our own social, economic, and political well-being
as a democratic nation. It is unlikely, however, that they can be couched
merely in terms of anticommunism or national preservation as some suggest. What we need, therefore, are positive objectives which will include
both our interest in the preservation of our traditional freedoms and way
of life as well as our interest in helping other nations achieve economic
and social progress.

Whether we like it or not, today the United States is a part of the
Inter-American Community and of the Atlantic Community. We must
think and act more in terms of community as opposed to purely national

interests. Our position has changed enormously over the past decade and can change even more in the next few years. Our nuclear monopoly is gone. Our economic supremacy has been whittled down. Our competitive position in world markets is being challenged as never before.

The question does arise also as to whether or not we are losing our world markets and whether or not we are pricing ourselves out of the market. Great changes are going on in Western Europe as mass production for a large tariff-free common market replaces production for small local markets. This development will inevitably narrow and may in time perhaps even eliminate the age-long productivity advantage the United States has held in many goods. And as the productivity differential disappears, so will also the wage differential. President Kennedy is correct, therefore, in proposing freer trade and asking for new trade and tariff legislation to replace the Reciprocal Trade Agreement Act. Some firms and industries will be injured, but the government should assist such industries to make adjustments.

Conclusion

In the opening paragraphs of this essay, I stressed the fact that economic systems are made from day to day to accomplish the economic purposes which men in their own time and their own environment deem to be good. This may involve a mixture of profit-seeking individualism and deliberate, governmentally organized activities — accomplished, of course, in a democratic manner. In this view, the state is the servant of man, not man the slave of the state or of the inherited institutions. This, I believe, is the dominant American view.

A certain amount of freedom may be lost in the pursuit of an economy that is free from the avarice of powerful groups, or one that provides some protection against economic insecurities, or is more stable. But it is important to distinguish between democratic and totalitarian restraints upon individual freedom.

Let me close with a paragraph from the bulletin of the Center for the Study of Democratic Institutions (The Fund for the Republic):

> Abundance will enable a reversal of the old order of things. Modern mercantilism will remove the economic machine from the middle of the landscape to one side, where under planning by inducement, its ever more efficient automata will provide the goods and services required by the general welfare. Humanity, with its politics and pastimes and poetry and conversation, will then occupy the central place in the landscape. Management of machines for human ends, not management by them, is the true object of industrial civilization.

This is the promise of modern mercantilism, and if the time is not yet, it is yet a time worth striving for. Meanwhile, the chief necessity is to revive respect for law and government as the proper instruments of the general welfare. Without this respect the economic future of this country and that of other nations linked to it will be determined, and stultified, by the accidents of private ambition and the hope of private gain. With this respect the Age of Abundance can be made into the Age of the General Welfare, and the United States can become in fact the moral commonwealth it has always claimed to be.

Comments

HENRY R. PEARSON

My analysis of Dr. Rasmussen's paper may be summarized in two points: First, he enumerates a succession of problems which beset our society; and second, he advances as the solution for the problems increased authority, intervention, and controls by government to prevent, to ameliorate, or to cure.

My reactions to Dr. Rasmussen's thesis may also be summarized in two points: First, the solution which he proposes will not work; and second, the solution would be undesirable even if it worked because the values compromised and lost would be infinitely greater than the advantages gained.

Dr. Rasmussen points first to what he terms the "growing power of the large corporations" which he apparently sees as a sinister threat to freedom, yet he applauds and proposes to expand the infinitely greater power of big government. It took more than one hundred years after the adoption of the Constitution of the United States for total federal, state, and local tax collections to reach the one billion dollar level. It took another forty-five years before the total tax burden reached the ten billion dollar mark. Then in only thirteen years tax collections rose to fifty billions. In another twelve years tax collections passed the one hundred billion dollar point. Federal, state, and local taxes required 12 per cent of the personal income in Utah in 1930, 20 per cent in 1940, 26 per cent in 1950, and 32 per cent in 1960.

Lest you rationalize that this enormous growth of government is primarily war or military in character, let me call your attention to what has happened since 1955. In 1955, the federal budget was $64 billion; for the 1962 fiscal year it is $81 billion. This is an increase of $17 billion or more than 25 per cent in eight years. The consumer's price index has risen 11 per cent in the same period, so that inflation fed by deficit spending is a significant factor. But national security expenditures account for less than $7 billion of the increase, while domestic nondefense spending increased nearly $10 billion during the same period.

The tremendous growth of government is only partly portrayed by the increase in taxes because we have been unable or unwilling to pay the bill for the governmental extravagance in which we have indulged. So it is that the formal national debt approaches $300 billion. That is only part of the debt story. If the debt and commitments of all federal, state, and local government agencies are added to that total, we are in debt $750 billion for goods already purchased or services already rendered. If unfunded obligations such as social security commitments are included, the total exceeds the trillion dollar figure. The federal government has operated at a deficit in twenty-four of the past thirty years, and the end is not yet. Two quotations from political sages of earlier years come to mind: "Heaven help a country when it finds it can spend the other fellow's money," and "A government that is big enough to give the people everything they would like is big enough to take from them everything they have, including their liberty."

For the most part, Dr. Rasmussen is obscure as to the connection between the problems of society which he cites and the growth of corporations. While he emphasizes the size of large corporations, he quotes Dr. Chayes of Harvard, who concludes his observations by saying, "What has been said amounts to no more than that the great corporation is the dominant nongovernmental institution of modern American life." The corporation has been perhaps the most important device of the industrial revolution, permitting the transition of society from the limitations of an economic system in which individuals produced primarily for their own consumption, to the growth of the marketplace economy, which accompanied the development of tools and mass production technology. The optimum size for efficiency has increased with the progressive complexity and cost of the tools of production. The growth of government, which has become the largest single customer of the large corporations, has been a very major factor in their growth. Only large corporations can handle efficiently the volume of contracts for goods and services which characterizes much of the military spending, for example. The sophisticated systems of electronic automation are designed for very large operations.

There is an unmistakable trend toward consolidation or termination of small business enterprise. But if your activity brings you into close contact with small business entrepreneurs as does mine, you know that the most frequent motive or cause given by these business men for the consolidations or terminations of small businesses is the inability or unwillingness to cope with the mounting burden of government regulation, reports, and restrictions, together with the proliferation of taxes which have first call upon any net income from the business.

Dr. Rasmussen complains that "in the modern corporation, the owner is, in general, a passive recipient, control is typically in the hands of management, and management usually selects its own replacements."

Surely, Dr. Rasmussen would not argue that stockholders or owners of business are more apathetic than the general citizenry, particularly with respect to the conduct of the national government. Dr. Lent D. Upson, dean of the School of Public Affairs and Social Work at Wayne University, wrote:

It is difficult to imagine a million small home owners or small business men, concerned with their golf, their backyard gardens or their appendectomies rallying to the battle cry of "economy and efficiency in public business." . . . I do not know the full answer of how to preserve democratic institutions which so many take for granted. Perhaps small possessors of democracy will eventually rise to the occasion when what they possess is seriously threatened.

Dr. Rasmussen's principal argument for the urgency of the problem of the power of large corporations is: "the recent revelations of misdoings by business: quiz-show rigging, price collusion, stock market manipulations, bid rigging, misleading advertising, etc."

Does Dr. Rasmussen mean to suggest that these revelations are peculiar to business, or that they are unquestioned proof of the evil of power of large corporations? I fully share the disgust which I believe all responsible Americans feel for these malpractices. But that they are justification for a further shift to more governmental intervention and regulation of the American economy, I do not accept. First, I would point out that governmental scandals through all of recorded history and including our own day, by both their frequency and their magnitude attest that transfer of responsibility for public morality to the government is not the answer. May I merely call to your attention the scandals which beset the Grant administration in the post Civil War era, Lincoln Steffens' revelation of the Muckrakers at the turn of the century, the Teapot Dome Scandal of the twenties, Boss Tweed days in New York or the Pendergast machine in Kansas City or Jim Curly in Boston, or Mayor Erwin or Brigham Street Pharmacy or Mr. Matthews in Salt Lake City and Utah and Salt Lake County governments, or the Orval Hodge multimillion dollar embezzlement from the state of Illinois, or the deep freezers in the Truman administration, or vicuna coats and Sherman Adams and Goldfine under Eisenhower.

Dr. Rasmussen notes the scandals which investigators have turned up in the ranks of organized labor. I submit that malfeasance and malpractice are the acts of human beings in every walk of life. They should be unmasked and punished in whatever field they are found. But the fact of their incidence in business does not warrant an indictment of the business system, nor suggest that government's role in the economy should be enlarged.

As for labor union abuses, I believe they arise from an artificial compulsion backed by government sanctions which deny workers the freedom of choice to join or not to join, to belong or not to belong to a union. If American workers individually were guaranteed these freedoms, then the responsibility of labor union leadership to the membership of their organizations would be restored, and the clean-up which most Americans, union or nonunion, want would be assured.

Dr. Rasmussen's commentary concerning assistance to particular groups appears to defend those subsidies most often criticized by the conservatives by chronicling the subsidies which have been given other groups, including subsidies to the critics. I shall not quarrel with the recitation nor the classification of either the early beginnings or the broadening scope of governmental subsidies. The most obvious fact about the effort to cure economic or other human ills by the use of governmental powers to take from one to give to another is that one subsidy inevitably leads to another, and we are fast getting into the position where nearly all groups must be subsidized. Grover Cleveland clearly saw the evils when he said, "It is the responsibility of the people to support the government, and not the responsibility of the government to support the people." Thomas Jefferson, author of the American Declaration of Independence, said, "We must make our choice between economy and liberty, or profusion and servitude . . . If we can prevent the government from wasting the labors of the people, under the pretense of caring for them, they will be happy."

The more serious aspect of governmental subsidies is that they do not accomplish the objective they seek; in fact, they more often aggravate the problem. The subsidies to agriculture, far from solving the problems of the farmers, have kept the market for agricultural products in turmoil and confusion, with wheat and dairy products stacking up in such quantities that just their physical care defies space and administrative ingenuity. Similar economic chaos marks the transportation industry, where subsidies to rail, motor transport, and the air lines are debated on the basis of reciprocal necessity. Even the subsidies seeking to alleviate human ills and suffering for individuals are accompanied by indications that dependency and unemployment are encouraged and made permanent for a growing segment of our people.

As for Dr. Rasmussen's allusion to Galbraith's thesis that the public sector of the economy is starved at the expense of the affluence in the private sector, I would point out that it is the growth of big government, and the pre-empting of ever-increasing shares of the income of the people for nonproductive governmental purposes which have dried up the sources of support for many of the functions listed. Most of these functions — schools, hospitals, slum clearance, urban redevelopment, sanitation — are the proper province of state and local government or of private financing. But with the federal government siphoning off so large a part of the taxpaying capacity of the people, there is nowhere to turn for funds. The answer is not expanded central government, but economy and retraction, and a return to the local agencies of the tax potential which local government services require. The availability of private funds for charitable, educational, or other eleemosynary purposes is limited by the growing presumption that government is doing or is going to do the job.

Dr. Rasmussen's third point concerns stability of the economy and full employment. Again his solution to the problem is more government and more regulation. I believe that the deadening, stifling hand of government controls and intervention, of oppressive taxation, including progressive tax rates maintained less for revenue than for ideological reasons, are the principal fetters which bind our economy. The providing of new jobs which requires more than $20,000 in capital investment for each new job created (and the figure is rising rapidly with automation) can most confidently be expected from new venture, new ingenuity, new products, better goods produced more efficiently. But this means greatly stepped up capital investment. But why venture, why risk when the government has first claim on more than half of the profit if you succeed, while you absorb all of the loss if you fail.

The greatest stimulus to human performance in the economic sphere is the assurance that the producer will enjoy the fruits of his own labor, his own enterprise. The fatal weakness of all collectivist plans is that neither force nor religious zeal will for long substitute for the inducement of reward directly commensurate with individual performance. That fundamental economic law has been diluted at the one hand by a tax structure which siphons a completely disproportionate share of the product of the most productive, and at the other hand by subsidies to the nonproductive which obscure the penalties for indolence or inefficiency.

The threat of big, insolvent government is the specter which arrests the dynamics of the American economic system which has been the productive marvel of the ages, and which is unrivaled in all recorded history in the bounty which it has made available to all strata of society. The scare of the alarming outflow of American gold reserves which has captured public attention is but a warning that international confidence in the soundness of the dollar is waning. Our unwillingness to place our governmental finance house in order could cost us our position of world leadership, and far more catastrophic, the loss of the human freedoms which are our cherished way of life.

Which brings me to my final point — even if more and bigger government were a workable solution to our economic problems, which it is not, it would still be the wrong course to take because freedom is more than economics. Freedom is the dignity of the human spirit, a divine gift and right which sets men apart from the animal creations. Dwight D. Eisenhower said this:

> Every step we take toward making the State the caretaker of our lives, by that much we move toward making the State our master.[1]

Herbert Hoover said it this way:

> Freedom conceives that the mind and spirit of man can be free only if he be free to pattern his own life, to develop his own talents, free to earn, to spend, to save, to acquire property as the security of his old age and his family.[2]

And John F. Kennedy, when a senator from Massachusetts, put it thus:

> The scarlet thread running through the thoughts and actions of people all over the world is the delegation of great problems to the all-absorbing leviathan — the state . . . Every time that we try to lift a problem to the government, to the same extent we are sacrificing the liberties of the people.[3]

And so, I would conclude with the wisdom of Somerset Maugham's words:

> A nation that wants anything more than freedom will lose its freedom, and the irony of it is, if it is comfort and security it wants, it will lose them too.

---

[1] *Commencement Address*, Columbia University, June, 1948.

[2] Herbert Hoover, *Addresses Upon the American Road* (Princeton, N.J.: Van Nostrand, 1946), p. 227.

[3] *Boston Post*, April 23, 1960.

ROBERT E. SMITH

Tonight I would like to comment on the relationship between political freedom and the economic role of government. I will assume that by political freedom we mean the regular election of representative officials and the existence of civil liberties.

It is a rather popular thesis among conservative and right wing spokesmen that there is an intimate connection between economic arrangements and political arrangements and that only certain combinations are possible. By one type of argument or another the possible combinations which involve political freedom are then normally narrowed down to one: the combination of a political democratic society and the free enterprise system which is based on private property, contract, and the competitive market. The least sophisticated of these arguments postulate that there are only two arrangements by which economic activity can be co-ordinated and controlled — the free enterprise system and government planning. According to this view, an increase in the economic role of government begins the inevitable slide into a completely planned economy, toward economic dictatorship. There is no middle ground. No political discretion is possible. It is as if political democracy contained within itself the economic seeds of its own destruction. The only safe course is abstention. To this theory of the inevitable slide into economic dictatorship is then coupled the proposition that political freedom must disappear in a completely planned economy because private property could not exist in such an economy and because private property is a necessary but not sufficient condition for political freedom.

Thus it is seen that this current equation of American Liberalism and the welfare state with Socialism and Communism rests on two arguments: the theory of the inevitable slide and the theory of the relationship between private property and political freedom. I am concerned tonight primarily with the first theory and with its implied assumption that there is no middle ground — that a mixed economy is not possible.

And this brings us to the main question: Do mixed economics exist? Are they characterized by political freedom? If they are now characterized by political freedom, are they in danger of losing that freedom and becoming communistic? I will attempt to answer these questions not by abstract reasoning but by reference to particular cases.

There are mixed economies. They include American, Canadian, Western European, and those of the Scandinavian countries. Are they characterized by political freedom? These are the countries which we recognize to possess political freedom. Are they in imminent danger of losing these freedoms? According to the National Education Program, an organization operating out of Hardin College in Arkansas and producer of "Communism on the Map," these countries are all lost to communism except Formosa, Switzerland, West Germany, and the United States.

Let us take West Germany as our case study. Not only is it still a free nation and safe from communism, but it also is frequently cited as one which we should follow because it is free enterprise in action. Let us, therefore, take a brief look at the West German economy.

Those who advocate West Germany as an economic model do so because it utilized a balanced budget and followed a "sound" money policy. It should be said that it was easier for West Germany to balance its budget because its military costs (including occupation costs) were below those, for example, of the United Kingdom. It should also be said that West Germany did not balance its budget from 1957 to 1960. The "sound" money policy, to the extent associated with a high interest rate, was somewhat fictitious in that the government manipulated some rates in order to direct investment, especially into housing.

But what about the rest of the economy? To what extent does it represent free enterprise and the operation of the competitive market? To what extent is industry nationalized in West Germany? Nationalized industries include the railroads, most local transportation, a large portion of the power and communication industries, and savings banks. Some manufacturing enterprises are also nationalized.

Is West Germany a welfare state? The United Kingdom is usually given as an example of a welfare state, but the value of welfare services in West Germany is 16 per cent of national income compared to 12 per cent for the United Kingdom. West Germany has a comprehensive program of compulsory medical insurance.

What about West German taxes? The combined governmental budgets of West Germany represent 35 per cent of the gross national product. This is estimated to be above all others in the West, including the United States, with the possible exception of the United Kingdom. The tax structure itself is relatively regressive. It is designed to increase private saving and to direct investment. An extensive and complicated system of tax discrimination influences the direction of the flow of investible funds and probably to some extent the volume of that flow.

At the heart of the free enterprise system is the private direction of investment. But as Wallich observed, a "good deal of planning took place" in this area, directed by the tax structure, and the "planning was valuable."[1] Investment was directed not only by tax policy but also by relatively direct investments by the government itself. It is estimated that between 1948 and 1957 about 44 per cent of domestic net investment was furnished by public authorities.

What has been the role of trade unions? Until recently they have not been active at the bargaining table. During the early fifties the goal of organized labor appeared to be the political one of codetermination. In 1951 and 1952 laws were passed under which the board of directors of each firm was to be divided between representatives of stockholders and of labor.

In fine, the West German economy has demonstrated considerable experimentation with and involvement of government in its economic decision-making processes. West Germany has sought a middle way as have most of the Western democratic countries. In fact, there are many middle ways as each nation, as if it were a laboratory, gropes to find its solution to similar economic problems. This is done within and preserves the democratic process. The political necessity is to preserve the necessary democratic values.

---

[1] Henry C. Wallich, *Mainsprings of the German Revival* (New Haven: Yale University Press, 1955), p. 157.

❺

Can We Educate for Freedom?

ASAHEL D. WOODRUFF

There are two pivotal words in our topic, *educate* and *freedom*. Educating is a vast and complicated social function. Freedom is a very complex state of affairs. With special reference to tonight's topic, both of these aspects of life are marked by considerable obscurity of meaning and no small amount of questionable thinking and irrationality. Tonight I am going to risk the charge of oversimplication by trying to handle this topic by means of an examination of phenomena everyone can see in life, rather than by attempting an academic analysis. I believe we can profit greatly from a look at what people do.

Let me begin with the suggestion that our problem is primarily a logistical one. We have something we want to get into a person. We need to determine the nature of the commodity we want to get into the person, so we can determine the specifications of the vehicle, and the route, for getting it in there. The topic implies that people are not behaving in a freedom-like way as much as we wish they would. Hence our objective is that of changing behavior. We have to talk about the content of education for freedom, and then the processes of education for freedom.

Much of the time we talk about freedom in very general terms, and this is satisfactory in many situations. We can talk about buildings in very general terms also; but before a builder goes to work, he must have definite specifications and blueprints. Hence we must describe freedom behaviorally. That is, we must try to say what people do which can be said to be the behavior of freedom. I see two kinds of behavior operating together.

The first is unhampered perception, choice, and achievement. A free person perceives without restriction, he chooses that which *he* wants, and he achieves his desires without running into obstacles he cannot surmount. This is the kind of thing Jesus was speaking of when he said, "Ye shall know the truth and the truth shall make you free." It is what Harold B. Medina had in mind when he wrote:

A liberal man must be a thinking man, one who has learned to evaluate his experience and the world about him independently and freely, using the ideas of others only as the starting points of his own analysis and creativity. . . .

89

He is always prepared to accept criticism and to try to understand opposing views. He constantly stands ready and is anxious to reappraise his own conclusions, ideas, and concepts of truth in the list of differing theories and new information available to him.[1]

The second is deliberate noninterference with the behavior of others. A supporter of freedom deliberately and consciously lets other people alone so they may be free and sees that such measures are taken as are essential to reach equitable compromises when the desires of two or more people require some restriction in their acts to keep them from trespassing on each other's liberty. This is what Patrick Henry may have been thinking of when he said, "Give me liberty or give me death." It is the message of the mottos of no less than eight of our states as exemplified by New Hampshire's "Live free or die."

The first might be referred to as having access to goals, and the second as the condition of being let alone. The first is an active search for satisfaction. The second is a deliberate restraint of interference.

For this discussion, I would like to refer to the first as freedom of access, and to the second as liberty. The terms are not important, but the ideas are very important. The two ideas, although they are distinct and separate notions and have to be examined individually, are inseparably interwoven both in their mutual effects and in the educational problem related to their attainment. Hence I want to make some observations about them. First, I will begin with the concept of "freedom of access," using that term in a generic sense, but I will also suggest some refinements which call for more specific terms.

Human behavior is not a gross, undifferentiated, conglomerate. It consists of numerous highly specific acts and combinations of acts, most of them directly aimed at self-satisfaction, and faithful to the values and realities of life as each person sees them.

Behavior in any full sense includes three processes: perceiving or sensing that which is around us, choosing from the alternatives that which we prefer, and doing what we have chosen to do. These three processes, so far as education is concerned, suggest the parallel ideas of "knowing of," "wanting or valuing," and "knowing how."

In parallel relationship to these three processes of behavior, we can speak of freedom to have vision or to perceive things one might want to seek, freedom to choose what one will try to do within the scope of his vision, and freedom to act or freedom to go to one's selected goal.

---

[1] Harold B. Medina, *The Anatomy of Freedom* (New York: Henry Holt & Co., 1959), p. 70.

Freedom of perception must be acquired by an individual through his own mental labor. Someone has said, "The eye sees only that which the mind gives it the power to see." This power has to be cultivated and won. To get it one must acquire a good bit of knowledge of objects, and circumstances, and understanding of the world. Then he must use some creative imagination. The finest visions we see are created by us; they are not just lying around waiting for us to see them. Freedom to perceive the good things of life is nonexistent for the uninformed and unimaginative. Freedom of perception may be affected by others, through the environment they create for the individual. In extreme cases, it can be severely narrowed by such means until the individual's breadth of perception is seriously restricted. It can be greatly broadened and stimulate wide perceptual development. In any case, each individual must do his own learning, or his perception will not rise much above mere sensory identification of the physical world around him.

Freedom of choice needs little comment. Personal choice made on the basis of personal preference is a process as natural and spontaneous as breathing. It needs no cultivating. It needs only protecting.

Freedom to attain one's goal depends on a number of factors. First, it is in a real sense a creative kind of behavior. It depends on the person's power to cope with the world. Obviously, it rests heavily on knowledge of many kinds, but in its best expression it depends also on the ability to analyze, to synthesize, and to apply intelligent imagination to the manipulation of things and processes. Next it requires discipline. The greater degrees of freedom of access are obtained by those with the greatest degrees of discipline. This kind of freedom demands that the individual immerse himself in the study of how things work in the world and school himself to conform to the natural forces and human tendencies he discovers through his studies. By conformity he becomes able to create. Even in art, discipline precedes creative production. Leonardo da Vinci said, "Those who are enamored of practice without science are like a pilot who goes into a ship without rudder or compass and never has any certainty where he is going." Similar expressions have been made by Albrecht Dürer, Jay Hambridge, and others.

Both freedom of perception and freedom of attainment depend heavily on education. Freedom of attainment also depends on the wise use by a society of policy power to protect liberty without, as Dean Adamson has pointed out, letting it go beyond this realm and interfere with freedom of access.

Freedom of attainment also requires intellectual honesty and the capacity to face criticism, to entertain suggestions while they are being examined, and to give up cherished positions and vested interests when impartial examination of a problem indicates that such actions can lead to progress.

If these are the elements of behavior which produce freedom, then we must provide in the curriculum for ways of producing breadth of vision, awareness of value, and large amounts of "knowing how" with their related competencies. We must also provide ways of cultivating sound creativity, internal discipline based on knowledge of reality, and a tough-minded intellectual honesty which makes a person face up to evidence even in potentially embarrassing situations. In addition, we must help people discover that it is really true that interferences with liberty cost us more than they can give, and that freedom is much more attainable when liberty is preserved than when it is not.

These elements of behavior are important to us in another way. The liberty and the freedom of access of any one person or group depend rather heavily on the way other persons and groups carry out their goal-seeking activities. But it is not just their goal-seeking activities we must examine, since these activities are guided by the individual's concepts of how people affect each other, and by his acceptance of the rights of others and his understanding that destruction of those rights will eventually destroy his own rights. If we have to educate people in these things, then we have to look at these human relationships to see the nature of our educational problem.

There is an intimate relationship between the technology of a culture, the conditions of freedom, and the role of education in maintaining freedom. As our society has developed, the conditions of freedom have changed. We must be aware of the nature of the change.

Professor Wormuth reminded us recently of the statement that freedom ended with the passing of the 40-acre farm per man. Let us look at this idea.

Liberty, or noninterference, was more prevalent when living space was less crowded than it now is. At least it was more prevalent for the head of the family. A man on his own 40-acre farm was not often interfered with by his neighbors. Under those same conditions, freedom of access to one's desires varied from person to person according to each person's knowledge, abilities, and material resources. It was severely restricted for everyone in those days, as compared with conditions today, by the limits of man's powers.

Two kinds of changes have occurred in America and elsewhere. There are more of us and we are getting closer together, and we have been developing technologically. As a culture becomes more crowded, it becomes more difficult for any individual to maintain his liberty unless each person voluntarily refrains from imposing on others. As the crowding increases, the degree of required self-control becomes greater. Each man's search for his satisfiers or goals tends to go beyond the limits of his personal uncontested living space and to invade the living space of others. More and more people find themselves hunting their satisfactions in the same places and competing for whatever they can find there. This gives rise to a need for mutual restrictions of liberty. As our society has developed, we have not developed evenly distributed restrictions, and we do not have mutually considerate ways of acting. Aggression, both of the laissez-faire type by individuals, and of the more pervasive type by means of law and policy power, has given the greatest liberty to the most powerful and aggressive.

Through our tremendous technological developments, freedom of access to goals has increased. With the increase in freedom of access to goals, it has become increasingly difficult to avoid infringing on the liberties and freedom of others. For example, my car operates most economically at about 60 miles per hour. If I always drive it that fast to satisfy my own economic goals, I will frequently encroach on the freedom of others. In fact I may kill some of them. This is the root of a problem equally as serious in my opinion as the problem posed by aggressive nations. Let me attempt to pursue it briefly.

In the process of cultural development, these things happen. First, workers acquire advantages by their intelligent toil. Second, some people inherit advantages from those who have produced and profited thereby. Third, some of the workers, but by no means all, encroach on the liberty and freedom of others and profit at the expense of others. It seems to me that it is morally right for a society to do what it can to prevent the encroachment of one person upon another, but that it is morally wrong or contrary to our concepts of liberty to try to prevent people from producing and enjoying the products of their toil, and from giving them to whomsoever they will.

By way of reaction to these tendencies, some more things happen. Some of them seem to me to be morally right. First, the have-nots sometimes get inspiration and go to work producing. Second, third parties, those who get concerned about their neighbors, seek to get those who have prospered in some way (intellectually, economically, spiritually, or politically) to engage voluntarily in extending help to the less prosperous. Third, they seek by legal means to prevent encroachment by one person upon the liberty and freedom of others. The more of these things we do the greater will be our combined liberty and freedom of access to our goals.

On the other hand, some of the reactions that take place seem to me to be morally wrong and destructive of our combined liberty and freedoms. First, the have-nots often try to take from others that which they have accumulated and appropriate it for their own use. Second, the third parties, and all of us are in this party some of the time, try by various means, legal and otherwise, to force those who have prospered to help. Often the third parties further their own interests in this enforced morality by taking out such dividends as financial cuts from the bounties they handle, by exploiting the have-nots through inciting them to riot or to wars to destroy or upset the prosperous ones and make their positions vulnerable, by themselves rising to status and power over others, and by capturing the hungry but naïve have-nots and using them in some form of controlled labor for the price of a mess of pottage.

I suggest that both organized groups and individuals among us are doing these things in varying degrees within our own local and national circles, that power groups of various kinds are doing these things on an international level, and that governments do these things both to their own citizenry and to other countries.

A genuine sense of dedication to the improvement of others has not been very prominent in the world and has certainly not been a force of any consequence in determining the way people affect each other, so in spite of its theoretical superiority as a way of life, we cannot explain human behavior or comprehend what is happening among us if we deceive ourselves into believing life goes along on such a basis. We must look elsewhere to account for most of what goes on among people that has a bearing on our concept of freedom.

As a move toward survival, an enlightened-self-interest form of moral consciousness begins to develop among those who have or who want liberty and freedom for themselves. To insure their own continued access to goals, they extend help to others to reduce the threat of interference, to increase the co-operative power of others, and also sometimes to achieve power and influence which will enhance their own freedom. This often tempts them to begin to encroach on the liberty of others in order to do the good which they believe will reduce the tensions. They easily go beyond the bounds of prevention of aggression, into an enforced moral philanthropy. This state of affairs involves all of us in a kind of compulsory righteousness and benevolence. It is often defended on the grounds that, although men ought to do good to the less fortunate on their own initiative, they do not do this; that the good must be done for the sake of the less fortunate, and hence that it is justifiable to use the political process to make them do it. This is a seductive and alluring idea, but when such force is used, one is entitled to raise a question as to the difference between legality and morality in the democratic process of government, and also the question as to whether such aggressive righteousness does the recipient good or harm.

Now I hasten to express a deep conviction that every man has a moral obligation second to no other to give all the help he can to his neighbors, and that he who does not do so is a very poor sort of person, if not a handicap to his society. At the same time, I believe firmly that certain conditions must always be present to keep this would-be help moral and beneficial. First, it must be recognized as a moral, and not a legal obligation. Second, the person who receives it must be ready for it, not just willing to take it. When we start to force men to do good, and when we create for a recipient a condition which seduces him into dependence, or indolence, or which causes his country to become embroiled in political chicanery and favoritism because of our unwisely given bounties, we defeat rather than support the cause of human development and freedom. It may well be asked whether in this process we buy comfort and security at the expense of liberty, and perhaps also at the expense of real progress toward freedom. Franklin said, "They that can give up essential liberty to obtain a little temporary safety deserve neither liberty nor safety." Robert L. Garner, President of the International Finance Corporation, recently spoke of part of this problem on the basis of many years of administration of foreign aid. He said:

I am troubled by the extent to which there is growing up the insidious consequences of too great reliance on foreign aid. There are too many instances where the obvious attitude is that the chief responsibility of a government is to secure the maximum help from abroad, with lesser responsibility to mobilize its own resources. . . . Money alone accomplishes nothing. It is only a tool. The effective spending of large funds requires experience, competence, honesty and organization. Lacking any of these factors, large injections of capital into developing countries can cause more harm than good. Economic development or the lack of it is primarily due to differences in people — in their attitudes, customs, traditions, and the consequent differences in their political, social and religious institutions.

Speaking in a similar vein, Herbert Thelen, a professional education scholar and critic at the University of Chicago, says:

As judged by what could be done if we were to understand and apply modern knowledge to educational problems, all our schools are obsolescent. . . . But most of this knowledge has so far made almost no dent at all on educational practices, and, with the present tendency to think that educational problems can be solved with money and organizational changes, the likelihood of any significant improvement is discouragingly slight. . . . I think our present situation is grave; more, it is immoral. For to act ignorantly when knowledge is available, to deny realities that patently exist and make a genuine difference is the worst crime of civilized man.[2]

I suggest that in this complicated society an uneducated and uninformed man has relatively little chance of keeping either his liberty or his freedom of access. In a highly technological society the man who does not keep pace in some productive way tends to become progressively useless, unwanted, and rejected. In the welter of human tendencies that are aroused and stimulated into aggressive behavior in the modern world, the man who is naïve about them will soon be taken over by the sophisticated.

Undoubtedly legislated law owes its origin to the recognized need for a set of enforceable rules against encroachment on liberty. As Burke said, "Society cannot exist unless a controlling power upon will and appetite be placed somewhere; and the less of it there is within the more there must be without."

But law has not been as successful an instrument for enhancing total freedom as we could wish it were. To the extent this is true, I believe it is due to the rather natural feeling some people have that any form of law is somehow in opposition to liberty, to the current feeling on the part of many that liberty requires the absence of restrictions on human ingenuity and industry no matter what direction they may take, and to the ease with which others among us fall into the assumption that anything we make legal by democratic means is *ipso facto* moral and harmonious with natural forces and laws. It is easy to become irritated with laws, because they obviously have only one intent, to make people do something or to prevent them from doing something, and this seems to some people to destroy freedom; but it is also easy to approve of restrictive laws when we happen to believe that they force people into what we regard as moral acts. As long as citizens on the whole are unclear as to the nature of freedom, it is unlikely that we can legislate wisely enough to guarantee the preservation and enhancement of freedom, or that even if we could, people could be induced to abide by the code.

---

[2] Herbert Thelen, *Education and the Human Quest* (New York: Harper & Bros. 1960), pp. 1–2.

Our way of life in America is a summation of the ways of life of all of our individual citizens, both as to our general cultural qualities and our political and legal structure. Therefore, law or no law, I see no great possibility of maintaining either liberty or freedom of access for all, except through universal education, with particular emphasis on the processes we must master to live in this culture, and on the human tendencies which operate both to enhance and to destroy our liberty and freedom. In addition, education has to touch the will of the person and not merely his understanding. Unless he chooses to honor the rights of others, understanding can become a powerful weapon for conquest. Armed with these two kinds of understanding and ability and with the will to maintain freedom, men can make decisions which will enhance freedom, but without them they will almost surely make decisions which will destroy freedom.

I have spent this much time examining human behavior to draw attention to the complicated nature of the subject matter of education for freedom, and to lead into the procedural problem that confronts us. It is difficult and complex.

Having referred earlier to the logistical nature of our problem, let me turn now from the effort to identify the rough outlines of the commodity to the matter of getting it into the individual so it modifies behavior. I would like to describe what I regard as sources of confusion in dealing with the processes of education.

The first source is our failure adequately to take into consideration the nature of the commodity of education. Instead of creating educational tools to match the nature of that commodity, we tend to invent a tool we like, and then imagine that every educative situation requires that tool. We are like the child Abraham Kaplan recently described in Atlantic City. Having been given a hammer for Christmas, he soon discovered that everything in his home needed hammering.

Statistics furnish a good example in the field of education. We have learned that a statistic which is to be used accurately and validly has to derive its nature from the phenomenon it is supposed to describe quantitatively, and not just from the logic of mathematics. The use of a Pearsonian product moment correlation on a set of data that have curvilinear qualities is a violation of this principle. Somehow we have not applied this principle sufficiently to research in psychology or to the processes of education. We still formulate research problems too much of the time on the basis of ideas about so-called mental abilities, or notions about how the brain and the nervous system work, and not enough on the basis of the phenomenon to which the brain and nervous system react. In education we have been unwilling to come to terms with subject matter, and see how *it* must be handled by the brain and nervous system. In reality, the brain is an astonishingly versatile organ which can do just about anything that is required of it by a sensory phenomenon in order to register the experience and utilize it at some later time in behavior. The key to what it does is very often to be found in the nature of the subject matter rather than in any *a priori* notion of mental processes.

Our commodity in education is subject matter. In spite of the irritation some educators display toward the stuff, it is still the central element in education. There can be no education without subject matter. There may be something else — child care, exercise, personality exhibition and cultivation, spontaneous expression of aesthetic feelings or of interests, but not education.

The term "child-centered" is a slogan which leads to confusion. A classroom which educates children cannot be child-centered. It is true that education must deal with children, but children must deal with that which they are supposed to learn, not primarily with themselves. Let it be "event-centered," with attention on the events that constitute the world and its life, and of course let it be appropriately matched to the child's capacity and readiness. The only course that can afford to be literally child-centered is the one in which the child is the subject of study.

The second source of confusion is our failure to recognize what is happening in human learning. Two educational processes have been going on simultaneously. One of them is currently referred to inelegantly by some social psychologists as "gut learning." A more appropriate term may be "empirical learning." Ralph Parlette wrote about it in *The University of Hard Knocks*. The other is formal education. Empirical learning is what happens whenever a person does something and finds out what happens as a result of it. It goes on largely outside of school, but a fascinating form of it goes on in school also on the side, and without much recognition or control by the faculty. Formal education tends to be confined to classrooms, and consists mostly of verbal learning of the content of written materials.

Empirical learning controls our behavior. We rarely disregard the messages of practical experiences. Formal education, on the other hand, tends to give us conversation material. We *do* those things that *life* teaches us to do to satisfy our wants and feelings. We *recall* that which we have learned verbally about things around us, when we want to *talk* about them.

The problem of freedom is concerned primarily with what we *do*, not so much with the way we *talk* — incidentally, so are most of the problems in life for which we have the deepest concern, as for example, our economic behavior, our religious behavior, and our social behavior.

Empirical learning has these qualities:

First, the individual sees something happening; often it happens to him directly. Second, he thinks about it, forms some kind of meaningful concepts about it, and draws some conclusions about it. Third, he tests his conclusions in subsequent events, either personally or by watching others, with two more results. The first is the correction of his concepts by experience and the consequent adjustment of his conclusions. The second is the acquisition of a sense of the value or effect which experience develops for each action he conceives and tries out, and the establishment thereby of motivation, either to do or not to do that thing again.

Formal educational processes have not had these same qualities, except in such academically disreputable classes as fly-tying, canoeing, cooking, basketball and industrial shop, and in the more respected science laboratories, student teaching, and a few other such event-centered programs. In these situations, students *"find out,"* that is, they get "know of," "want to," and "know how," because they are getting ideas from real events and testing them empirically.

At this point we must recognize that man is capable of symbolic behavior in which he can deal with reality in the abstract. This is true, but herein lies the crux of our educational problem. He can do this *only* after his physical senses have delivered to his brain the basic sensory data with which the brain can make mental constructs, and not before this happens. Once he has the basic sensory data and organizes it into meaningful concepts, he can invest his ideas with value, that is, he can suppose that if he acts in a certain way, a certain result will follow. To get beyond the supposition stage, however, he must engage in the behavior and get back from it the message of his own feelings as he is rewarded or punished by what he does and what it causes the world to do back to him. This process is clearly described by Harry Broudy in his *Building a Philosophy of Education.*

Laboratory-type classes are more like the empirical-learning processes than any others. As we move into our logically organized bodies of subject matter, we lose progressively the possibility of teaching them by the empirical learning processes. Why? Because subjects are translated from real events in nature to symbolic marks on pages, and they are arranged no longer in the natural flow of events from which they were discovered, but in abstract and logically categorized form. What remains as a possibility, then, is to learn the printed symbolic version, and this calls for the mental process of memorization. Memorization does not affect concepts. It is a relatively detached mental process at a different layer in the brain, so to speak.

Let us look at the kind of subject matter which is central to liberty and freedom. It is largely in the area we call the social sciences. This is the most highly verbal area of our whole curriculum. It is notoriously the most difficult to teach and the most poorly taught. It is also the area in which everyone feels he is an expert because it is about him and what he does. It is characterized more than any other area by popular myths, and by wishful misinterpretations of fact.

The social sciences (economics, sociology, psychology, political science, social anthropology, and others) are studies of the way man acts and what happens among people by way of ramification and echoing reactions to his acts.

This leads us to the third source of confusion which consists of some difficulties that beset us in the field of the social sciences. The difficulties operate in our efforts to see what is happening and to understand it. They give rise to misconceptions by individuals at the empirical learning level which cause them to form conclusions that are often contrary to the facts which are taught in our formal verbal courses.

One of these difficulties is found in the dangerous hallucination that people can be led to do good to others through self-denial. This is contrary to psychological facts. Regard for others is not the original *cause* of considerate behavior; it is the *result* of it. The outstanding exception to this is the typical mother's love for her child. The real cause is enlightened self-interest. The individual wants more physical, social, and personal satisfactions. He has to get others to provide them in greater abundance. To do this he must help them obtain satisfactions so they will produce. At the same time he must make himself valuable in their eyes. This requires helping them obtain what *they* want. That is impossible unless he knows what they want. He can't know much about them unless he develops a certain amount of intimate acquaintance and receptivity to their ideas. Intimacy of acquaintance usually breeds understanding, discovery of admirable qualities, sympathetic response, and finally identification and love. This constitutes a broadening of the self by inclusion of others, not a denial of self in favor of others. It is the exemplification of the teaching of Jesus. "Thou shall love thy neighbor *as* thyself." Self-interest remains dominant but for a larger self. The thing that limits this process is the lack of intimate contact with others. When we persist in trying to get people to do good because it is morally right, we are wasting time and money. We had better begin teaching people that their own well-being depends on how much good they can do for others.

A second difficulty consists of the illusion that verbal codes control behavior. We have two rather discreet levels of behavior. The verbal or symbolic level consists of memorized ideas and their oral or written expression. The functional level consists of the often unrecognized input from gut learning. It controls what we do. This fact, too, is often unrecognized by us. These two levels of behavior may and often do contradict each other. The functional patterns are not affected by verbal activity. Most people are unaware of their functional patterns, and of the diversity of these patterns from their verbalized mental content. They do not realize, either, that their behavior follows the functional, not the verbal pattern. Man presents us with a curious paradox. He is the highest form of animal life because of his more advanced brain. His crowning feature is the part of his brain which makes language and symbolic behavior possible, but it is this feature which tends to obscure his awareness of the internal mental processes which record the meaning of experience and use it to control purposive behavior. Our whole educational program is caught in this illusion, so we use our verbal facilities to teach each other and require verbal responses to check on the learning, most of which produces no effect on the functional patterns of our behavior.

A third difficulty consists of the element of time and its effect on human observation of events. Human beings exist in a time range of minutes, hours, and intermediate units up to a few years. They are capable of perceiving the relatedness of sequential events only within a limited time range. Most of the natural laws upon which intellectual, social, and economic progress depends operate over a much longer time range than human beings can perceive without special training. Periods in the neighborhood of several generations or even historical eras are required to see the final effect of violation of many social laws. Some show up in shorter periods. Economic effects of various kinds of fiscal policy may appear in shorter periods but still extend beyond the perceptual capacity of most people. Hence, the typical individual fails to connect circumstances with their real antecedent conditions. In the absence of such insight, he proceeds to rationalize by using the little and immediate circumstances and arrives at deceptive conclusions.

Social scientists and philosophers have developed the ability to make these ultra-time-range perceptions. They begin then to see what is happening. They try by verbal means to teach us what they see and promptly fall into the same old verbal difficulty mentioned earlier. Our blindness causes us to think highly of acts which seem productive when looked at within a short period but which may really be destructive when judged in terms of a generation or more. The problem here is how to telescope these slow movements so they can be perceived by others than trained social scientists.

The social scientist can overcome these difficulties, but the student cannot. The student reads the scientists' conclusions, but lacking his own sensory data he cannot interpret the verbal reports. Conversely, he has his own experiences to draw upon, in which he suffers from the difficulties just named. Thus many a boy has learned that it pays to steal because of his continued success, whereas stealing will in the long run and throughout a culture destroy more than it yields. The boy learns verbally a set of formulas about social life which he does not really believe or comprehend. At the same time he learns empirically a set of personally tested behaviors in which his own senses have given him only partial facts, and his interpretations have suffered from delusion due to the difficulties I have tried clumsily to describe.

Can education escape from these traps and difficulties and purvey realism to students? Yes, it is possible. In conclusion I should like to state what I believe are the conditions on which it can be done.

First, I would name the recognition that subject matter is the center of education, and that it must be the point of attention all the way up the ladder.

Second, I suggest that we must set up the kinds of learning experiences which involve empirical learning and not verbalism. This requires that for every concept we try to teach, we must arrange things so the student can see the thing happen, can think about it and come to an understanding of it, and can then test his concepts for validity and for the sensing of value. Some of this, perhaps much of it, can be done vicariously, but not through the avenue of words in logical subject-matter packages.

Much in the recent developments stemming from Dewey and Progressive Education is wholesome in so far as it frees the child from excessive formalism and encourages him to use his powers fully. In my opinion, however, we will have trouble achieving the goal implied in tonight's topic unless we make certain adjustments.

We should give up the clinical orientation which exists today in many elementary schools based on Freudian concepts of mental health. Children are treated as if they could not stand either direction from teachers or demanding standards of performance. Most of them are not sick, and they do not need this therapeutic form of teaching.

Decision-making *per se* on the part of a child in school is not going to make him wise or develop his creativity and independence. Everyone makes decisions all day long, and everyone is not a well-developed person. It is not that a person has made decisions that has made him into something; it is that he has made certain good decisions consistently, and on the basis of understanding, and particularly that he has been taught or has learned by himself those things he must know in order to carry out his decisions.

We should turn away from the unstructured basic curriculum, wherever it exists, which leaves to children the decision on what they want to study, and bring to them instead a carefully selected curriculum of facts known to be of vital importance in human affairs. Certainly the curriculum must make provision for self-selection by all students of lines of study which hold special interest to them, but this must be supplementary to the basic essential curriculum required in our culture, and not in place of it. In schools which now have a pre-planned curriculum, and most of them still do, we should choose the contents on the basis of some priorities based on their usefulness, and get rid of some which are now included.

We should transform our subject matter from the sterile lists of topics, which now constitute most of our courses of study, into life-oriented concepts of natural forces and human tendencies that shape and affect our lives.

We should adopt in teaching the simple but essential processes which enable a student first to perceive; second to think about and comprehend what he has seen; and third to test it, verify, or correct it, and get the sense of value which will transfer it from an idea to a motive and a tendency to act.

Coming directly to the problem of freedom again, the curriculum must include the facts about all of the ways in which our human tendencies draw us into infringements on the liberties of others, and of the ways in which we must act to preserve our liberties against the long-range foreclosures of unwise short-term expedient acts. Finally, we must try to educate every person so he can hold his own in productivity in this marvelous modern world. We are not now doing these things well, but we can if we have the will to put ourselves through the necessary discipline to accomplish them.

America is a sweet land of liberty, to be sure, but if it is to stay so, we must understand that liberty is not a self-perpetuating condition. We will remain a land of liberty only to the extent that we individually acquire much understanding of the human tendencies that mitigate against liberty and much knowledge of the processes by which we can achieve our aims; to the extent we commit ourselves deliberately to values we have accepted thoughtfully, and actively oppose values we have rejected knowingly; and to the extent we have acquired the discipline needed to follow our chosen values at whatever cost may be involved in energy, firmness of purpose, and resistance to opposing forces. For this we can educate if we will.

Comments

ESTHER R. LANDA

When Dr. Read called many months ago and asked if I would participate in this series as a commentator, I hesitated to accept; for I felt that as much as I was dying to make the big time, I would surely be out of my league in this series. Last week as I was reading Dean Woodruff's paper and came to that sentence which read "the use of the Pearsonian product moment correlation on a set of data that have curvilinear qualities is a violation of this principle" then I *knew* I was out of my league. But the earlier temptation to try to dispel some commonly held descriptions of school board members was so strong that I could not give Dr. Read a negative answer.

This is an unaccustomed role for a school board member. Like children of the past, we are supposed to be seen and not heard — at least on anything that might have to do with educational philosophy. A good school board is supposed to hire the best superintendent and staff it can find and then let those people do the philosophizing and set the directions for the education of the children of the district. Admittedly, school board members are generally conceded to have some limited competencies. For example, we are supposed to be capable of dealing with such things as real estate matters, selling school buildings — buying them back — purchasing equipment and supplies, and so on. But here I was with a chance to get into the field of philosophizing, so I accepted.

At the outset may I differ, perhaps sharply, with Dean Woodruff on a few points, and then examine where we might be in agreement. I was stopped abruptly in his very introduction with his use of the word "logistics." I did not like it, maybe because I thought it was a military word, and we have been having some trouble with them lately. So, consciously or subconsciously, I rejected it because I had always thought of education as a bringing-out process, as a developing, an evoking thing — as defined in the dictionary from the verb *educe*: to bring about, to draw forth, to elicit, to evoke, to develop.

In his seeming anxiety to get away from an endorsement of the so-called child-centered school, Dean Woodruff insists throughout on the subject-centered school. I think what he is really talking about, however, is a process-centered school. By what process do we get the subject matter into the child? That question seems to be his main concern. I do not think that the so-called child-centered school concept ever made much headway in this country. Certainly it is not present in our school systems today to any degree. Oh, there was a time a few years ago when I remember one of our kids coming home and reporting: "Oh boy, is that teacher dumb!" "What's the matter this time," I asked. "Well," was the reply, "she asks us all what we want to do, and she writes it all down on the board and then we do what she wants to do." I haven't had any reports like that lately. As Dean Angleman said last week in a quote (I believe it was from Chesterton) about Christianity — "the only trouble is it has never been tried." I feel somewhat the same way about progressive education — it was never really tried under the proper circumstances. But that is history now, and I repeat that in my opinion today's schools are not child-centered in that sense. I would buy Dean Woodruff's definition if he would broaden it to describe a child-subject-process-centered school.

What I have always felt was important about progressive education was its emphasis on treating each child as an individual. To me this was an application of the Judeo-Christian ethic which says each human being has a potential for good, that having been created in the image of God — whatever that is — he is worthy of dignity and respect and should be allowed and encouraged to develop to his highest potential. And I had been taught that this was good. I feel that Dean Woodruff has either overlooked or did not have time to develop in this paper what I would deem one of the best ways to educate for freedom. And that is by having education carried forward in a free, democratic atmosphere. What kind of school system does the district seem to be running? What kind of school is the principal running? What kind of classroom atmosphere is the teacher creating?

I believe that the good teacher creates the kind of atmosphere in which children can learn because they are being treated as if they were free human beings, capable of learning, capable of achieving, capable of thinking, capable of solving problems, capable of reasoning. The good teacher really believes this and treats pupils in this manner. This is not a master-slave situation, but a situation in which pupils can learn the most difficult subject matter as well as the easier.

You see, if it were just a matter of logistics, we could have a teaching machine-factory school. I understand that one of the research corporations in California has planned just such a school. It would be completely equipped with teaching machines and would require only three human beings to staff it: an administrator, a physical education instructor, and a janitor. I hope that school is still on the drawing board and has not been built. I am glad my children are not in such a school. Children so educated or trained could conceivably come out with a lot of information, but will they know what to do with it? And what kind of society would be created by the products of such an educational system?

We *can* educate for freedom if the school, personified by the teacher, *believes* in freedom. Sure, the "kids" have to have subject matter. For example, they have to know not only the words of the pledge of allegiance to the flag but what those words mean, and I see no harm in having all, except those who object on religious grounds (and foreign exchange students), repeat this every day. But this is only the barest beginning of the process of building free citizens who can contribute to a democratic society. In a democratic society children have to acquire skills, and if this is what Dean Woodruff means by subject-centered, I agree.

Now to conclude with comments which have to do with the school children themselves. Dean Woodruff says that a clinical orientation exists today in many elementary schools. "Children are treated as if they could not stand either direction from teachers or demanding standards of performance. Most of them are not sick," he says, "and do not need this therapeutic form of teaching." He is right: most of them are not sick. We would say that over 90 per cent of them are not sick, but we would say further that these over 90 per cent *are* getting direction from their teachers and that they are meeting standards. The standards may not be and are not as high as we would like them to be, but we are constantly trying to elevate them. But we would also estimate that there may be about 10 per cent of our students who could benefit immeasurably from clinical mental health facilities, and we would like to have enough skilled social workers and psychologists to identify these children and to be able to help them to perform to standards and realize their potentials.

Now quickly to two other points. I miss in this paper any discussion of what the educational policies commission of the N.E.A. and the A.A.S.A. in their latest statement call the central purpose of American education: the development of the rational powers of man. Perhaps Dean Woodruff was as flabbergasted as I was to read this, coming from that particular group, but they now say that it is the rational powers which enable a person to be free, and to achieve his goals. They say it is the development of the ability to think which must be the central task of the school. In Dean Woodruff's "gut learning" situation, there is not much discussion of "thinking." My question is: could not the something happening in the gut learning process he describes, could not that something be the result of the use of rational powers, that is, the result of the learning of an idea or a concept? In other words, is personal experiencing on the functional level the only way to learn? I am sure Dr. Monson is much more qualified to comment on this point and perhaps he will help me out here.

Dean Woodruff devotes quite a bit of his paper to the idea that too many laws and too much charity spoil man for freedom; and perhaps there is much to be said for this point of view. However, there is a converse view which should be stated. We do need to educate people toward freedom; but nothing helps to get the point across like a good old law. I recall Rabbi Podet testifying on this point at a legislative hearing on a civil rights bill introduced into the last Utah legislature. He said: "We who honor law look to the majesty of the law to protect the rights of all, to point out to the uncertain the proper way, to frustrate the unfair, and to encourage those who would support and sustain the vision of America's founders."

Dean Woodruff questions the difference between legality and morality in the democratic process of government. The other view is that the law should embody the *highest* morality of the community. Again, if what he is saying is that individual responsibility is the inevitable and indispensable partner of privilege and right, I would say "Amen." I liked Dean Woodruff's explanation of enlightened self-interest. It follows a saying of Hillel, the great Hebrew sage of the first century, "If I am not for myself, who is for me? If I am only for myself, what am I?

And if not now, when?" But it is difficult for me to reconcile Dean Woodruff's advocating "we had better begin teaching people that their own well-being depends on how much good they can do for others" with his earlier statement about compulsory righteousness and benevolence. Do not voluntary righteousness and benevolence need to be channeled into proper directions? At least it seems to this naïve observer, for example, that those institutions which advocate tithing seem to accomplish more than those which sporadically pass the collection plate.

Could not we admit, though, that in the realm of our political institutions as long as we maintain a representative system with free elections, we must be willing to abide by the decisions of our elected representatives. I have often been chided by colleagues on our own board of education who say: "Now, Esther, do not go too far on that." And I always reply, "Gentlemen, I wish to go no farther than the Congress of the United States tells us to go in legislation signed by the President of the United States which, to this moment, has not been repudiated by the Supreme Court of the United States."

In conclusion, I agree we should do away with whatever unstructured basic curriculum still exists, if any, and that we should transform our subject matter from a sterile list of topics to life-oriented concepts. I suggest that one of the first places to do this is in the teacher-training courses, and especially in that in-service education of teachers which we on school boards emphatically and urgently would like to see meet the actual needs of the teachers as they see them on the job, and not as unrelated credit hours which can be picked up in evening classes.

I am in hearty agreement with Dean Woodruff's conclusion that the curriculum should include facts about the ways in which we may, and do, infringe upon the liberties of others, and, especially, about the ways in which we must behave to express positive concepts of freedom and liberty.

CHARLES H. MONSON

I believe that Dean Woodruff's paper is a most valuable addition to this year's discussion concerning freedom. I say this confidently because I agree with much of what he says.

In particular, I recognize the distinction between freedom of access and liberty and agree that in our own time we are achieving more of the former than of the latter. I agree that concern for the means to achieve the end is as important as the definition of the end, and that education is one of the prime instruments in achieving the goals recognized by a free society. Moreover, I share the opinion that in our educational theory and practice we have been too ready to impose the techniques of quantitative measurement on the question of mental achievement and value, failing to recognize, as Dean Woodruff says, that the brain is "an astonishingly versatile instrument," and failing, as well, to heed John Dewey's oft-stated admonition: "To suppose that scientific findings decide the value of educational undertakings is to reverse the real case. Only actual activities in educating test the worth of the results of scientific findings." If I might pause for a moment to illustrate the seriousness of this point, not too long ago a young man came to me with a proposal to write a Ph.D. dissertation in educational philosophy, and, as part of his procedure, he proposed a questionnaire, to be given to my colleagues in the department, from which he could tabulate and classify answers to be put into a chart. I'm certain that statistical data have their values, but *not in deciding what is valuable,* especially when the figures are an attempt to report such elusive qualities as attitudes and beliefs.

And I also share Dean Woodruff's concern regarding the influence of Freudian thought on education. Reacting against the Victorian period, Freud rightly pointed to the consequences of childhood repression and provided a liberating influence for child development; but, as Erich Fromm points out, Freud's battle has been won, for the most part, in our world today and yet mental illness is still with us. Perhaps repressed libidos and crushed egos are not as important as we once suspected, although it is my impression that this concept is not as important in educational practice as many of the contemporary critics of education would have us believe.

However, there are two points in Dean Woodruff's paper I wish he had not written, or, since he did, I wish he had not said, but since he did, I am afraid I shall have to criticize. The first concerns his argument regarding liberty; the second, his comments regarding what he rather indelicately called "gut learning." On the first point I want to contend that on Dean Woodruff's own premise a different conclusion should have been drawn, and on the second, that he has failed to make a proper estimate of man's nature.

At the beginning of his paper, you recall, he distinguished between freedom of access, the ability of a person to make and act on his own choices, and liberty, the principle of noninterference with the freedom of others. He then pointed out that liberty was more meaningful when living space was more plentiful. But he then went on to argue that legally or politically enforced limitations on liberty were morally wrong, only voluntarily recognized limits being justified.

I would suggest that this conclusion is subject to doubt both on the grounds of practicality — for as Dean Woodruff points out, most of us cannot extend our view of time sufficiently long that our self-interest becomes truly enlightened — and also on the grounds of the preservation of freedom. For while freedom as liberty might have been diminished, freedom, as freedom of access, as a matter of fact, has been increased. That is to say, if freedom is taken to mean the ability of a person to choose from among competing alternatives, then men are infinitely more aware of diverse alternatives and the advantages and implications of each than they used to be. Far from lamenting the loss of freedom as liberty I think Dean Woodruff should be praising the increase of freedom as the opportunity to make intelligent decisions based on an informed understanding of a diversity of alternatives, whether or not that kind of freedom has been achieved by legally and politically enforced rules. What we have lost in the principle of noninterference, then, has been more than replaced with an increase in the freedom of access, the opportunity and ability to make and act on intelligent choices.

My second point concerns "gut learning," for I want to say a few words in favor of verbal or what I think I shall call "the aching brain" kind of learning. Dean Woodruff praises gut learning because it is meaningful, controls our behavior and is remembered, and he downgrades aching brain learning because it leads only to memorization. My objection is simply that verbal or symbolic learning is not to be equated with mere memorization. Through verbal learning man can know vicariously of situations before he experiences them, and hence can judge intelligently whether he should experience them or not. Moreover, his and his ancestors' experiences can be generalized, put into symbolic form, transmitted verbally and thus provide the guidance for individual behavior. Without this guidance, we would be forced to repeat our ancestors' mistakes continually. As Alfred North Whitehead has said: "Those who do not know history are forced to relive it."

This is only to say that Ernst Cassirer was right when he said man was a symbolizing animal, and that one of the important points in education, then, must be the transmission of symbols. This enables us to direct our future activities intelligently and to learn from our own and other's mistakes and, moreover, encourages the creativity Dean Woodruff so warmly applauds. To acquire this kind of learning, however, requires an aching brain instead of merely a pained intestine.

However, I would like to conclude my remarks on a constructive note, one which I think is in harmony with Dean Woodruff's general thesis. Freedom is neither a gift nor a right; it is, rather, an achievement. It is a condition which has resulted from the confluence of certain historical events: the contract theory of the state, the doctrine of nature law, the principle of brotherhood, the rise of the common law and others. As the forces which challenge this achievement change, so, too, the conditions necessary for its preservation must change.

At the present time, education is one of the vital forces which can help to preserve and extend what Dean Woodruff calls the freedom of access. By perpetuating our knowledge of the past, by disseminating information concerning alternative courses of action, by increasing an awareness of the challenges to, and conditions necessary for, freedom, and, above all, by trying to foster a sense of individual initiative, personal responsibility, creativity, an intelligent concern for making reasonable and justified conclusions, education can be not only the preserver but the chief preserver of the conditions necessary for freedom to exist as a high and valued good.

Of course, freedom implies diversity and diversity results in disagreement, so in addition to fostering the ability to make intelligent choices from among alternative courses of action, education also must convey the idea that a diversity of choices is a sign of vigor and health, and that a freedom in which all people reach the same conclusions and act in the same way is no freedom at all.

In my view, then, the function of education in a free society can be stated quite simply. It is to teach history, in the broadest sense of the word, encourage intelligent responsibility, and foster tolerance. The degree to which education increases these qualities is one of the prime factors determining whether we will pass on to our children the achievements of a free society which our parents passed on to us.

6

What Freedom Is Found in the Local Culture?

WALDEMER P. READ

Ladies and Gentlemen: You may as well sit back and relax. You have not been invited here to be told that the Danites are on the prowl. We are here to talk about a quality of mind, the conditions of its development, and its significance for human life and values.

It may interest you to know that in planning these great issues programs, all members of the staff of the Department of Philosophy work together as a committee of the whole. When planning the current series, we quite readily agreed upon the general theme: great issues concerning freedom. When we began listing possible particular questions to be discussed on each of the several evenings, it was soon discovered that we were agreed one question that should surely be considered was the one we are concerned with this evening. Moreover, each one seemed quite ready to write the paper. The consequence was that I suddenly found myself "drafted" for the job. I left the planning conference in a state of high exhilaration. But the next morning I was sober again.

Why? I asked myself. Why should I have the affrontery to talk to my own people about their bondage? If I feel that I must examine a specific culture, why not choose that of Cuba, Formosa, Communist China, East Germany or Spain? It would be different, of course, if I were about to take a slow boat to China — if I had accepted a position with the University of Calcutta or Teheran, or if for some other reason I contemplated leaving these valleys of the mountains; but, since I am not contemplating any such move, why not let sleeping people lie?

Just when I was engaged in these reflections of uncertainty I heard for the first time the sound of the Nauvoo bell, and heard the enthusiastic explanation by the television announcer that throughout the world, wherever this bell is heard by persons who know its history, its tones will have a special significance. It rings for freedom!

Now this surprised me, to say the least. A very significant claim was being made for the local culture. Uncertainty about the propriety of my assignment eased. Since such a claim of special significance for the culture is made, it is surely admissible that the appropriateness of that claim be reflected upon. My reflections have been as follows.

I

I must begin by mentioning freedoms that are so taken for granted that we are apt to forget them. In Utah we enjoy the political and civil liberties that are characteristic of America. No *lettres de cachét* are issued here. There is no Bastille nor even a Tower of London. The rack, the pillory, and the stake are gone. Bills of attainder are not allowed and the individual enjoys the protection of the writ of habeas corpus. There is no gestapo in Utah nor secret police, and no concentration camps. Though there is, in fact, the mission field, calls to which have occasionally been given to young men showing signs of dereliction. In fact, people come and go as they please; they meet where they like if they like; they read what they like—sometimes with the advice and consent of their spiritual leaders; they say what they like; they do what they like without fear of molestation. There is little doubt but that most people of Utah regard the freedoms they enjoy as ideal for the world.

However, the freedoms I have mentioned are not distinctive for Utah. Rather, they are characteristic of America as a whole. With respect to them we but participate in the common American heritage. In themselves they scarcely justify the distinctive claim made for the Nauvoo bell. Such justification would seem to require that this culture and its people have a greater than usual appreciation of these freedoms, and a greater than usual zeal for their protection, preservation, and enhancement. It has been my impression that such has not been the case.

An evening might well be spent in documenting this impression of mine; however, I must content myself with one or two brief remarks to indicate its nature.

I think the record will show, for instance, that during the rise of naziism Utahns were not distinctively clairvoyant nor concerned with respect to the nature and seriousness of its threat to freedom. On the contrary, reports came from missionaries laboring in Germany and from the president of that mission — reports amounting almost to boasting — that though the Catholic and Protestant clergies were having difficulties with Hitler, the Nazis saw nothing in the activities of the Mormon missionaries to alarm them. In retrospect it would seem that this fact of history can be reconciled with the claim now made for the Nauvoo bell only if the freedom for which the latter tolls is understood to have an eschatological (i.e., an other wordly) reference and to have nothing to do with the political freedoms and civil liberties of the here and now.

It is my opinion that McCarthyism has been the most serious internal threat to freedom to which Americans have been exposed, during the last half century at least. As a distinctive bulwark against this menace, the local culture has nothing or little to its credit.

I am convinced that an examination of the record would reveal that in regard to this matter local leadership, including both church and press, was woefully silent. When politicians in Utah, as in some other states of the Union, made effective use of the principles and tactics of McCarthyism to win elections, they were not rebuked.

I resist the temptation to write this record in detail and to give documentary support, for our chief interest here this evening is with another aspect of the problem of freedom. I have alluded to the above matter only to underscore my demurrer to the claim that the local culture and leadership has been distinctively zealous and valiant in defense of freedom.

I realize that some will want to remind me that it was a senator from Utah who took the lead in the Senate action to censure Mr. McCarthy. But even in this, little credit goes either to the leadership in Utah, to the senator from Utah, or, for that matter, to the United States Senate for manifest concern for the political freedom and civil liberties of the individual citizen. In the first place, the act of censure came belatedly — after the successful candidate for the presidency of the United States had taken McCarthy by the hand and welcomed him as a fellow-traveler on the road to political victory in a campaign in which resort was frequently made to McCarthy-like appeals and charges. In the second place, the act of censure when it came was not taken in defense of individual freedom but to preserve the integrity of the United States Senate — or, more accurately, to preserve the integrity of the majority party in the United States Senate. In the third place, the act of censure-ship was directed at Senator McCarthy and not at McCarthyism. McCarthyism, in fact, went uncensured — unrepudiated. This is probably a chief reason why it is still with us — ready, once again, to raise its ugly head.

I repeat: with respect to these matters I am not contending that Utah was more culpable than other states; but, merely, that she was not less so. Her leadership might have acted with distinction; but it did not.

II

I turn now to the more central problem of the evening. The question, "What freedoms are found in the local culture?" raises a prior question: "What freedoms are conceivable?" In partial answer to this, let us begin with Thomas Hobbes' observation:

Liberty, or freedom, signifieth, properly, the absence of opposition: by opposition, I mean external impediments of motion; and may be applied no less to
irrational and inanimate creatures, than to rational. For whatsoever is so tied,
or environed, as it cannot move but within a certain space, which space is
determined by the opposition of some external body, we say it hath not liberty
to go further. And so of all living creatures, whilst they are imprisoned or
restrained, with walls or chains, and of the water whilst it is kept in by banks
or vessels, that otherwise would spread itself into a larger space, we use to say,
they are not at liberty to move in such manner, as without those external
impediments they would. But when the impediment of motion is in the constitution of the thing itself, we use not to say it wants the liberty, but the
power to move; as when a stone lieth still, or a man is fastened to his bed by
sickness.

I propose to take issue with Hobbes' rather limited conception of
freedom; but before I do so, let us note the various freedoms that may be
distinguished within the scope of his conception — a conception according to which anything is free in the degree to which its movement is
determined and limited solely by its own nature, and unfree in the
degree to which its movement is determined and limited by factors
external to itself.

In the first place, there is a physical freedom, as exemplified by the
stone lying still in the plain or rolling down the mountainside, and by
the water descending along the stream bed. I suppose Utahns share this
freedom on equal terms with everything else in nature. Secondly, the
freedom of vegetation may be noted. Consider a garden array of sweet
peas — how every tendril, every leaf, every flower has placed itself, in the
very act of growing, in response to the conditions of the environment —
how this freely growing array contrasts with what you have when the
rude hand of man seeks to thrust the plants into a posture not their own
and succeeds only in producing an awkward disarray. Sweet peas freely
growing seem to forget and, indeed, obscure from the beholder the
trellis which sustains their posture. Each flower gives forth a sweet
radiance of individual loveliness — complete in itself — a perfect individuation of the species to which it belongs.

A sweet pea differs from a stone, Hobbes would say, not in freedom
but in power. It can do what a stone cannot.

I suppose Utahns can be said to enjoy a kind of sweet-pea freedom —
and in this they share with all growing things. A human analogue to
the individual blossom of the sweet pea might be seen in the young
maiden freely going to Sabbath school — her raiment clean and brightly
colored, her hair neatly waved, wind-blown or ratted according to her
taste, the bloom of youth on her cheeks concealed by just the right

amount of drugstore luster, and the thoughts she will think that day carried in a manual in her hand. A perfect specimen of her kind!

But then there is also animal freedom. Consider the wild deer — unconfined yet keeping to its range, foraging at will, and lying down to rest in favored places. On second thought, perhaps it is not the wild but the domestic animal whose behavior is a fitting figure of our freedom. We are allowed to roam at will; but we will to remain fairly close to home and always — except on rare and special occasions — return to the home at night or at least toward morning. We sleep in our own beds and do it gladly. The normal Utahn is housebroken; and he drives along the right-hand side of the street, not under restraint, but willingly. Having been disciplined to right action, he finds that conformity comes easily, naturally. As has been said, "We teach our people correct principles and let them govern themselves."

If you are beginning to feel irritated by these remarks, and for the right reason, then I have accomplished my purpose. We are not here to discuss the freedom of rocks and rivers and sweet peas; nor of animals, whether wild or domestic; but human freedom — the only freedom worthy of the name. Human freedom is freedom of the mind.

I began with Hobbes' conception of freedom because I wanted to emphasize the inadequacy of that conception. This is an important thing to do since Hobbes is quite popularly followed—by all those who equate freedom with liberty and conceive them both in negative terms, as consisting essentially of the absence of external restraint. For Hobbes a rock is as free as a human, if equally unrestrained. The two differ, not in freedom, but in power. It is this attempted separation of freedom from power that is at fault. Hobbes went astray here as a consequence of the basic assumption that underlay all his thinking, namely, that the categories of physical science are adequate for an account of all phenomena.

Avoiding Hobbes' error, I turn to the conception of freedom as a positive characteristic of the agent. Of two men in a burning building, one able to flee to safety and the other disabled by paralysis, the former has the greater freedom. Of two men picking cherries, one standing on his own two feet while the other, legless, is held aloft by a short ladder, it is the first who picks the more freely. Ability to prosecute one's desires is a condition of freedom. And since increase in ability to execute, that is, to effect, to do, gives increasing latitude to desire it also increases freedom. Other conditions being equal, therefore, the literate man is more free than the illiterate; he who can cipher is more free than he who cannot; and all increase in mental powers is an increase in freedom.

Thus the phrase "education for freedom" is not meaningless; and it means more than merely education for certain political, juridical and social forms.

I come now to a certain aspect of this mental or intellectual freedom: it is the dimension of freedom with respect to which I wish to characterize the local culture. Other conditions being equal, that individual who can think new thoughts — thoughts that no one before has thought — is freer than those who cannot. Moreover, that society whose membership includes individuals who can think new thoughts is free — and is free to a degree which varies directly, one would think, with the proportion of its membership having this capacity. Other conditions being equal, then, it is inimical to freedom both in the individual and in the collectivity for there to be too great a degree of channelization, stabilization of the patterns of imagination, of conception, and of judgment and belief. Excessive stability in these matters is the foe of creativity; and, by the same token, it is the friend of the *status quo,* of sameness, monotony and death. The importance of these considerations cannot be overemphasized. Let me get at the heart of the matter by reading the words of a contemporary scholar,[1] words appearing recently in the *British Journal of Aesthetics*:

Let me define value . . . in terms of unconditional vitality . . . vitality is the power of enduring or continuing. Hence, if it is vitality, value should not simply be equated with life in its actual manifestations but rather with the fountain head of life, i.e., with power rather than with the manifestations of power and, since perpetual endurance of the actual *status quo* degenerates into stagnation, [value should be equated] with creativity or advance. Value is not life but a trend of life which is not exhausted however exacting.

The reason for opposing vitality to life is that life in the broad sense of the term includes stagnation and waste. Even death, the extreme form of waste, is said to be a facet of life. But surely frustration or death excludes value. It is because men know waste or destruction to be at the root of evil that they equate the good, or value, with vitality.

And let me continue with words from one of America's outstanding contemporary scholars, Wm. F. Albright:

A group may be so completely integrated that it exhibits little internal friction, a high degree of efficiency in accomplishing its purposes, together with self-sufficiency and smugness — but it will accomplish little of value for the world. The early Christians were certainly not well integrated as a group, since it required centuries for them to come to a temporary agreement on normative theological doctrines and social policies — yet few will dispute

---

[1] A. P. Ushenko, "Pictorial Movement," *British Journal of Aesthetics,* Vol. I, No. 2 (March 1961).

their potential capacities for good. Modern Jewish intellectual circles are generally as fine examples as can be found in history of lack of integration, yet they are producing an astonishingly high proportion of the significant intellectual achievements of our age. It is even possible that the greatest advances in any group are made when that group is in the highest state of excitation that can be attained without disaster to the group. All this obviously means that there is most likely to be progress within a group when that group contains an optimum number of polar elements, i.e., of elements standing in real or potential opposition to one another.[2]

And now listen to the dean of living philosophers, Bertrand Russell:

. . . those who believe that the voice of the people is the voice of God may infer that an unusual opinion or peculiar taste is almost a form of impiety, and is to be viewed as culpable rebellion against the legitimate authority of the herd. This will only be avoided if liberty is as much valued as democracy, and it is realized that a society in which each is the slave of all is only a little better than one in which each is the slave of a despot. There is equality where all are slaves, as well as where all are free. This shows that equality by itself is not enough to make a good society.[3]

And again:

Ever since history began, the majority of mankind have lived under a load of poverty and suffering and cruelty, and have felt themselves impotent under the sway of hostile or coldly impersonal powers. These evils are no longer necessary to the existence of civilization; they can be removed by the help of modern science and modern technique, provided these are used in a humane spirit and with an understanding of the springs of life and happiness. Without such understanding, we may inadvertantly create a new prison, just, perhaps, since none will be outside it, but dreary and joyless and spiritually dead.[4]

One is led to recall that great classic in modern literature, John Stuart Mill's *On Liberty*, which is an eloquent appeal for freedom of thought and speech, freedom of action, taste and pursuit as essential conditions for freshness, vigor, vitality, and the continued enrichment of the life of the human spirit. Mill quoted Von Humboldt in support of the idea of individuality "as one of the elements of well-being": " 'individuality of power and development': that for this there are two requisites, 'freedom, and variety of situations' and that from a union of these arise 'individual vigor and manifold diversity,' which combine themselves in 'originality.' "

---

[2] William F. Albright, *From the Stone Age to Christianity* (paperback, New York: Anchor Books, 1957), pp. 105–6.

[3] Bertrand Russell, *Authority and the Individual* (paperback, Boston: Beacon Press, 1960), p. 48.

[4] *Ibid.,* p. 51.

We are concerned with more than aesthetic richness and vitality, important though these are. We are concerned with increasing the likelihood of the alleviation of human suffering and misery and of the enhancement of the conditions of life and health. Indeed, it may well be that we are concerned with a critical factor having to do with the very survival of the human race. It is not yet manifest whether or not the race is going to annihilate itself within the next month, year, decade or century. Whether or not it does may depend upon our ability to come up with some right answers to the problems of our times.

III

From these considerations it follows that we are concerned with much more than freedom of imagination and conception. Also vital to our well-being is independence of judgment and belief. If we are fully free we must be capable of intellectual discrimination. In the words of the late Lyman Bryson, we must be able to distinguish between "significant truth," "plausible falsehood," and "beguiling half-truth." This is a task for intelligence, for "competent inquiry." Our freedom here is a function of our ability.

What, then, are the marks of competence in inquiry? What are the essential features of that method which has been slowly evolved through long centuries of groping and travail — that method which has proved effective in the discernment of truth, the achievement of knowledge and understanding — the scientific method? I mention three features: the power of conceptualization gives wings to the imagination, and freedom in conceptualization is the unfettering of those wings.

But conceptualization is not cognition. Concepts are not knowledge but merely the stuff of knowledge, the material means. The second important feature of the method, therefore, is the recognition of the distinction between the true and the false. Many, however, are aware of this distinction, and even concerned about it, who lack any clear notion of how to sort out the true from the false. They lack what might be called an adequate sense of evidence; i.e., a sense for what sorts of considerations should guide the attempt to identify the true. It is not clearly recognized, for instance, that belief is not in itself an indication of truth; that is, that subjective certainty is of no evidential significance. Though we always have to act on faith, i.e., on belief, in the quest for truth, faith is no substitute for evidence. Faith usually amounts to nothing more than a psychological state of satisfaction with received beliefs. Nor is the comfort which an idea gives a mark of its truth. Ideas, like husbands or wives, though false may be comforting. This is a hard lesson.

In fact, only two sorts of considerations are legitimate for the identification of true propositions. Notice I say, "for the identification of true propositions," not beliefs. When we undertake to separate true from false beliefs, we are dealing with materials where prejudice (i.e., faith) already has a "weight" advantage. As a student wrote recently on a test paper: "It is with this question as it is with so many questions in this class: though there is no evidence for my belief, and though it is contrary to reason, yet it just seems that there is something more — by which I know the belief is true." I repeat, only two sorts of considerations are legitimate for the identification of true propositions: considerations of empirical fact, and of logical relation. The history of science shows that these are the two legs on which science walks. Why is it so hard to learn this lesson — to learn it not only in theory, but in practice?

IV

For an answer to this question we must turn to a consideration of the possibilities, methods and devices for the control of human beings through a control of their minds. Thought control is by far the most effective kind of human control.

Three or four years ago a man made a splash for himself by publishing a book discussing "hidden persuaders." In that book we were told of the possibility of our being told to "fly United," "repeal the income tax," or "smoke Lucky Strikes," without knowing we are being told. The eye being quicker than consciousness, we may be indoctrinated by messages frequently flashed on the screen for such brief instants that we are unconscious of them. The eye can receive the message without our seeing it! Moreover, and this is the important point, suggestions lodged without our knowledge will be effectively accepted. This latter is assured provided only that the unseen flashes affect the eyes and nervous systems at times when, and under conditions such that, the mind (organism) is in a receptive mood. People became alarmed about the possibility of their being taken advantage of by unfair devices in advertising. Indeed, what's to prevent the complete enslavement of the nation by a modern Pied Piper?

A generation before this scare Huxley, in his *Brave New World*, had prophesied the use of phonographs concealed beneath the pillows of sleeping children as a means of instilling group loyalties. A night-long playing, softly so as not to awaken and yet loud enough to be heard, of some such repetitive refrain as "I am a Mormon boy — I am a Mormon boy — I am a Mormon boy" was certain to have its effects.

The more sophisticated among us were not frightened, however; for we knew that since the beginning of human society men and women have been committed to beliefs, policies and practices without knowing why they were committed. Moreover, for generations men have studied, both in logic and in psychology, the mechanisms back of these commitments. It has long been known that most beliefs are not reasoned; they are caused. They are effects, not conclusions. This is to say they are not freely espoused, and cannot be freely laid aside. Of course, given the beliefs, men are always ready to reason in defense of them — and so the term "rationalizing" has come into vogue. "Rationalizing" means "finding *good* reasons as opposed to the *real* reasons for believing or doing what one is going to believe or do anyhow."

For generations elementary textbooks in logic have carried a warning against a large class of fallacies generally designated as illegitimate appeals to emotion. (In logic that phrase is redundant.) The essential nature of this group of fallacies is this: that by the arousal of the emotions the critical faculties are thrown off guard, the attention is diverted, and the idea which is being advanced by the fallacious argument gets past the censor without being examined for its credentials — and, once accepted by the mind it will be defended by the mind. The case is not dissimilar to that of the person crashing a party, who, once he gets by the doorman, is accepted as one of them by the guests and by the hostess.

Time permits that I merely mention only one of these fallacies, the one so predominantly used by modern advertising — the fallacy of special pleading. This is exemplified by television's use of charm, in the form, for instance, of a sweater girl, to sell tobacco, drinks, light globes, men's deodorants, and limousines. Frequent is the time that one finds oneself, just from viewing television, "fairly fit to be tied" — ready to buy anything, from moth balls to heavy farm equipment.

The trick is to present the commodity or idea to be sold in association with some lure — in fisherman's language, the hook should be present in, though concealed by, the bait. A nice balance is important. Statements about the merits of the commodity, arguments in its behalf are submitted, but it's the lure that makes the logic palatable. More correctly, little logic is involved; the appeal is psychological.

Psychologists will recognize that what we are talking about is the conditioning process as it is employed in advertising. For nearly three quarters of a century textbooks have carried accounts of the "conditioned response." Though this term is associated with the name of Pavlov, actually the manipulation possibilities to which it refers have been known and talked about for centuries. Modern behavioristic psychologists did not originate the phrase: "Bring up the child in the way he should go, and he will not depart therefrom." The laws of learning talked about in associational psychology, which, incidentally, dates back to Thomas Hobbes and before, are causal laws.

So here we have it: in logic, special pleading; in psychology, conditioning: twin names for the same process — a process logically invalid though psychologically effective. This is the process back of the tenacious adherence to beliefs that cannot be intellectually justified.

V

I hope you will pardon this recital of the commonplace. I have engaged in it because of the critical relevance of these considerations for our problem. What I have hoped to emphasize is that the conditioning process is a means of manipulation, an instrument of control. Moreover, the conditioning process is equally effective whether used unwittingly or with deliberate intent.

The bearing of this principle upon our problem is simple. Individuals become members of society, not through reasoning, but by conditioning. Every institution, every family group for instance, and every church group is a conditioning agency. Through conditioning it recruits and controls its members.

In order that any society may function well, its members must acquire the kind of character which makes them want to act in the way they have to act as members of the society or of a special class within it. They have to desire what objectively is necessary for them to do. Outer force is replaced by inner compulsion, and by the particular kind of human energy which is channeled into character traits.[5]

Now this is not a bad thing — and I am not against it, any more than I am against the weather. In fact, man may be defined as the institutional animal; and, as a matter of fact, therein lies his freedom. Were it not for institutions the members of the species Homo sapiens would be mere animal organisms, frequenting the breeding places and the sources of food supply, preoccupied with each other's bodies, with gustatory and olfactory delights, with momentary quarrelling, and with slumber. We couldn't even have a good war.

---

[5] David Riesman (ed.), *The Lonely Crowd* (New Haven: Yale University Press, 1950), p. 5, quoting Erich Fromm.

However, institutional control is like rain, or food; it is good up to a point; beyond that point it is deadening. Institutional control is good if the institution which provides it is open at the top; if the institution is closed, then the control is bad. That is, an institution may be such as to provide a ladder by which the individual may reach a launching pad from which he may transcend the very forms that lifted him; or, it may provide a ceiling which shields him, to be sure, but also limits him and uses him as one of the elements in the truss which holds it up. Institutions of the first sort liberate the human spirit; those of the latter kind imprison it. Bertrand Russell has written of the harm in educational systems which treat the individual child as a means to an end, not as an end in himself. "The teacher," he says, "should love his children better than his State or his Church." To so love the child is to want to liberate him. It is to refuse to treat him as mere plastic material to be molded to a common form; it is to cherish his individuality, his uniqueness, his independence of thought and belief, his potentials as a possible contributor to the growth and enrichment of the human spirit in the continuing progress of mankind.

I come now to the task of the evening: the characterization and assessment of the local culture in the light of the foregoing considerations. In what follows I shall endeavor to make two points: 1) that the controls in this culture are excessive; and 2) that they are unfortunately so.

What, then, are the features of the culture which make for control and render it unlikely that any new ideas will prosper here?

The first thing that should be mentioned is the fact of stifling uniformity in belief. Doctrines are standardized. Even the defense of doctrine is routine. Contrary to there being "an optimum number of polar elements, i.e., of elements standing in real or potential opposition to one another," there is almost no disagreement. Imagination is not stimulated and judgments are not challenged by conflicting opinions. No one challenges the other. Rather, the belief of each reinforces and sustains the belief of others. A common feature running through the programs of all of the many organizations is a remarkable pattern of continuous rehearsal of familiar and accepted beliefs. This, I repeat, is in contrast with the condition requisite for the cultivation of freedom; namely, diversity of opinion, making possible habituation in the search for and examination of possible alternatives — I say examination of possible alternatives — something distinct from the self-protective *noting of inferior* alternatives.

As features of this complex of uniform beliefs and teaching practices, certain methodological beliefs are noteworthy. These beliefs tend to reinforce the uniformity. They become matters of attitude and function in the culture much like a governor functions in a locomotive or motor bus. They tend to insure that no discussion will get out of hand, that no heretic will run away with the argument, that *The Truth* will always prevail. Three of these attitudinal or methodological beliefs are: 1) belief in the absolute certainty of the doctrine (the dogmatic attitude); 2) belief in the wickedness of doubt; and 3) belief in the authoritative hierarchy. All three of these beliefs are conditioned responses. No one of them can be justified as an aid to cognition. They all tend to block inquiry, or, rather, to transform inquiry into rationalization. Of all of the beliefs which characterize the culture, none are more carefully cultivated than these. A word or two, therefore, about each.

Dogmatism is inimical to freedom in thought. It denies the need of inquiry — save the inquiry of the learner; it denies the need for further research. In contrast with dogmatism, science became successful when it became tentative, sceptical, self-corrective. The scientific spirit is one willing to settle for probable as opposed to certain truth. But for the scientist no settlement is final. He wants to be as assured as possible; and that induces a willingness to look again, to re-examine. Dogmatism in its very nature is unreadiness to re-examine. It transmutes reason into "right reason"; right reason is that which comes up with the accepted answers. It has little in common with that reason of which Russell spoke when he said:

Men fear thought as they fear nothing else on earth — more than ruin, more even than death. Thought is subversive and revolutionary, destructive and terrible; thought is merciless to privilege, established institutions, and comfortable habits; thought is anarchic and lawless, indifferent to authority, careless of the well-tried wisdom of the ages. Thought looks into the pit of hell and is not afraid. It sees man, a feeble speck, surrounded by unfathomable depths of silence; yet it bears itself proudly, as unmoved as if it were lord of the universe. Thought is great and swift and free, the light of the world, and the chief glory of man.

Turning now to the adoration of faith and the distrust of doubt which characterizes the culture, it will be well to remind ourselves of remarks of John Stuart Mill: ". . . it is the opinion men entertain, and the feelings they cherish, respecting those who disown the beliefs they deem important which makes this country not a place of mental freedom." "No one can be a great thinker who does not recognize that as a thinker it is his first duty to follow his intellect to whatever conclusions

it may lead." The free mind recognizes that the question of truth —
the determination of truth — is prior to the obligation to believe. The
insistence upon faith begs the question of truth. The local culture penal-
izes the reluctant believer by holding him suspect as to character. Too
frequently, it is assumed that an attiude of scepticism or of unbelief is a
sign of moral turpitude and of spiritual rebellion. For too many, the idea
that an unbeliever may be a good man is quite unthinkable.

Perhaps no theme is more popular with Conference speakers than
the importance of deferring to the authorities in matters of judgment —
not only with respect to doctrinal interpretation, the reading of the
scriptures, but with respect to matters of policy and practice. Social
wisdom is supposedly vested in the Brethren — and deep moral insights.
"When those who are in authority have decided, the thinking has been
done." The virtue of deference to authority is thought to be one of the
strongest assurances of salvation. It is, however, an abnegation of individual responsibility in thought. When carried to extreme, it is the
antithesis of freedom of mind.

> If thou seest a man of understanding, get thee betimes unto him,
> And let thy foot wear the steps of his door.
> Yet accept no person against thine own soul,
> And let not reverence for any man cause thee to fall;
> But let the counsel of thine own heart stand:
> For there is none more faithful unto thee than it.
> For a man's mind is sometime wont to bring him tidings,
> More than seven watchmen, that sit above in a high tower.
>
> — *Ecclesiastes*

Dogmatism, adoration of faith, and deference to authority: all three
of these conditioned beliefs tend to solidify and perpetuate the uniformity of belief.

A third factor of control is the rather highly articulated ideology
which characterizes the culture. The rather remarkable body of doctrines expounded in authoritative books and scriptures makes it possible
for a believer to appeal to basic principles and purported facts, to make
deductions, and to come up with conclusions. Such a believer gets the
sense, therefore, of having derived his beliefs intellectually, and of being
able to defend them intellectually. But this is all within the system —
which system itself is not usually questioned. One begins with the
acceptance of the scriptures as authoritatively interpreted in the books,
and from there on all is clear sailing. Not many members, therefore, are

fully aware of the extent to which their conclusions rest ultimately upon psychological rather than logical grounds, nor how fundamental to their own position is that of St. Anselm, who said, "... I do not seek to understand that I may believe, but I believe in order to understand. For this also I believe, — that unless I believe, I should not understand."

The fourth feature of the culture which makes for excessive control is the very monopolistic nature of the program — the very thoroughness with which it is developed. The home, if it is functioning as desired, is a conditioning agency for the church. Moreover, every ward with its meetings and ward suppers, every auxiliary with its socials, its lessons, dances, celebrations, testimonials, and fellowship, every fireside meeting, every seminary and every Church Institute, each with its fellowship, its socials, etc., the church-wide basketball league, the annual dance festival — each and every one of these, and the persons functioning in them, is a conditioning agent dedicated to the psychological sale of the central beliefs — including those methodological beliefs which make for unity. The aim is psychological conditioning in allegiance to the Church as an authoritative institution. Toward this end there is a persistent attempt to get every individual involved for as many of the waking hours of his life as possible in church activity — even, often, at great cost to other legitimate interests of the individual, such as school work. The great emphasis upon attendance drives which has been characteristic of recent years is eloquent evidence of the deliberate nature of this conditioning program.

I make no sweeping claim that these various activities lack intrinsic worth, nor that they do not, often, have instrumental worth in promoting the fine things of life. My claim is merely that the conditioning function of the activities should not be overlooked, and that this function is a major reason for the sponsoring of the activities.

Finally, one should recognize that the very success of the culture is a source of its controlling power. It has so established itself in the minds and hearts of the members of the group, it so fills their lives with meaning, purposes, and satisfactions that to them it seems but good sense to cherish faith, respect authority, and participate co-operatively in the program of mutual indoctrination. What if it is a practical and emotional orientation, rather than intellectual — as practical and emotional it pays big dividends.

It is true in this culture as in all others: of the cords that bind the minds of men and thus limit their freedom, it can be said that they do not chafe or gall as did the chains in the ancient dungeon, or those that bound the ankles of the ancient galley slave. Rather, they warm and comfort. The sweetness of the bondage is its greatest strength. It must have been of these slaves that Rousseau spoke when he said, "they love their servitude."

VII

If though there is excessive control the people like it, if they love their bondage and prefer security to freedom, why, then, should it be thought unfortunate?

One answer to this question is in terms of the inevitable monotony that must result from a successful perpetuation of the *status quo*. If the actual *status quo* cannot be preserved without a resulting stagnation, then we would seem to be headed for Russell's "new prison, just, per- haps, since none will be outside it, but dreary and joyless and spiritually dead." We can scarcely wish to see all life become a mere "waiting for Godot." But this is not the point on which I wish to dwell.

The fact is that the *status quo* cannot be preserved. However unde- sirable, a static culture in a static world is at least thinkable; but this is not a static world. The times are pregnant with change. Whether we like it or not, on the morrow things will be different — how different we do not know; but old things will have passed away and new things will have emerged. Whatever else may be said of the forces that are being loosed in the world today, they are forces of destruction. To expect to survive their impact without change is unrealistic.

There never was a time when the world, and, particularly the United States, had greater need for new ideas. This need is critical. What is uncertain is whether the changes ahead will be unanticipated and cata- strophic or intelligently foreseen, prepared for, and directed. What is to be regretted, therefore, is not that the local culture is geared to preserve its theology, but that in being so geared it is incapacitated to contribute needed new insights and conceptions bearing upon national policy and action. Moreover, it is likewise incapacitated to *support* new insights from whersoever they may come; and this also is regrettable.

I shall close this discussion with an enumeration of ideological hin- derances with which the people under the local culture are saddled and which militate against the likelihood that they will contribute anything of significance to the solution of the problems that confront this nation and the world. I will mention four obstructions, not necessarily in the order of their relative obstructiveness. I regret that time will permit only that I list them, without development and without defense.

1) Utah is tied to an antiquated doctrinaire economic conservatism which, though it is consistent with the business-corporation mindedness of the church, incapacitates the people for constructive participation in the solution of urgent problems having to do with human well-being.

2) Utah has a built-in isolationism which prevents enthusiastic participation in efforts to establish world peace. The lukewarmness of this people, including its leadership, toward the United Nations, for instance, is but a consequence of its theology.

3) What may be called "exclusivism" — the "we are right and so you are wrong" attitude — requiring as it does that the world be made over in our image is an obstruction. Those who believe that world peace will come when and only when the peoples of the world all believe and worship as we do attach too much importance to conversion. In contrast, the vision in the scriptures is of a time when the lamb and the lion will lie down together, and, presumably, not after the latter has eaten the lamb. This is a vision of peaceful coexistence, which calls for an achievement of peaceful relations under conditions in which the distinctive values of each culture are preserved and protected.

4) The last obstruction that I will mention is our built-in racial prejudice. No problem is more critical for our future than the racial problem, unless it be the problem of population, of which it is a part.

One could wish that our contribution to the solution of the urgent problems that now face us and that lie still unseen in the future could be something more than "foot-dragging," but such would require a quality of inner freedom that we do not have, and that we are not about to develop.

Comments

DAVID W. BENNETT

I have learned by what has occasionally been sad experience that many wonderful subtleties lurking in Dr. Read's colorful manner of expressing himself are apt to miscarry and produce an effect opposite to the one he intends. It is easy to mistake Dr. Read as a man who is as subtle as the flying bricks for which he is so rightly well known. I would like to begin my remarks tonight by spelling out a point which I believe Dr. Read wished to make, though I risk destroying the subtle humor of his manner of making it. He says that all of us in the Philosophy Department were agreed that one question which should surely be considered in our forum series is the one we are concerned with this evening and that each of us seemed quite ready to write the paper. The truth of this matter is that my colleagues and I have in the last several weeks been testing out various ten-foot poles by which to handle, even then reluctantly, tonight's subject. No one of us has been more conscious of the delicate character of tonight's topic and more cautious, or, in a phrase well-loved in this culture, more humble in approaching his task, than Dr. Read himself. Some listeners here tonight, understandably unsympathetic to his paper, are apt to disallow his genuine expressions of reluctance to do what he has done and to take at face value his description of the "state of high exhilaration" in which he began it. I believe in his opening paragraphs he was trying modestly to convey to people like me whose lives have been conditioned by the local culture that exhilaration was not his mood and that he wished he might avoid offending us.

What Dr. Read has said is not offensive to me: in fact the greater part of it I would like to have said myself. He has underscored certain undesirable features of our culture which have been embarrassing and disheartening to me and many of my good Mormon friends for a long while. In spite of this I am very sensitive to the fact that what he has said will be offensive and unpalatable precisely to those people whom he hopes to benefit by his remarks. There are people here tonight who have told me they were coming for the pleasure of seeing the Mormons get a good roasting. I suspect that Dr. Read could not care less about such people. As a good pragmatist he does not talk to fan the air and create a breeze. It is not worthwhile to say anything about the local culture just for the amusement of the profane; someone must benefit from hearing what is said.

Now I can think of people who *could* benefit from this paper, but I do not think it likely that they will. If I know my own people they will be moved, but in the wrong direction. Some of them will be offended and angry. They will feel misrepresented and misunderstood. This will entrench them more deeply in their own culture and make them more distrustful of its critics.

What I am suggesting is that when you hope to change beliefs and practices of people through constructive criticism you must first get their confidence. Once you have won this you can go surprisingly far with them; without it you can never get started.

Would it be possible to point out the kind of thing Dr. Read has been pointing out in a way which will not offend and anger us? I believe this can be done. I will have time only to suggest two or three examples. Dr. Read notes the dangerous loss of individual freedom which results when people follow their leaders too closely and relinquish the right to make their own judgments. This danger has also been noted in public addresses of many of the authorities themselves, including presidents of the church. Dr. Read notes a widespread belief in the wickedness of doubt, though I fear he has further entrenched this belief among those who cherish it. Now this unfortunate doctrine of the wickedness of doubt can be much more successfully undermined from the Mormon scriptures themselves than from a heretic like John Stuart Mill. Again one can point to general authorities and even presidents of the church who have publicly owned up to their own doubts and have emphasized the importance of doubting in the search for truth. Dr. Read notes that for too many the idea that an unbeliever may be a good man is quite unthinkable. How true! But how many times have the Mormon people been warned by their leaders against judging their fellow men? How easy on the basis of Mormon principles alone to refute these notions.

I think I can anticipate Dr. Read's reply to these comments. "True," he may admit, "Mormonism at its best will agree with me on these and perhaps many other points I have made. I am not talking about Mormonism as it may rarely be found among its saints or near saints, but rather as it appears in the large, among the vast majority of the people who are under its sway." Now if this is his reply I do not think he is playing fair. An institution, particularly a religion, ought not to be judged only by its average product, but by its highest fruits. The average is bound to be pretty uniform from one religion to another where proselytes are sought from all classes of society and where large numbers of people are involved. The question is whether out of these multitudes a significant number of free individuals can emerge and can do so with the help of rather than in spite of the church. On this criterion I think I have no reason to be ashamed of my people. Of course I count Waldemer Read and many others among the elect who would be disqualified from this title both by themselves and by the church they have abandoned. I count some of these avowed heretics among the highest fruits of Mormonism. This seems only fair on the grounds of Dr. Read's example of members of the Jewish intellectual community, many of whose ties to the more orthodox religious forms are similarly remote.

I can only take time for one further point. I suspect in the church there is a much higher state of internal excitation and a far greater number of the polar elements necessary to progress than appears on the surface. Some of these polar elements are implicit in the doctrine and everywhere in evidence in the practice of the church: for example, individuality *vs.* conformity, education *vs.* indoctrination, security *vs.* eternal progress, freedom *vs.* authority.

Some of my friends will say after these remarks that they cannot tell which side of the fence I am on. In my ears this is high praise. I am for tearing down all the ugly religious fences which men have built to segregate themselves from their neighbors. True neighbors do not need fences, at least not ugly ones without gates. I believe that the most fruitful attitude to take towards other men's religions is the sympathetic attitude. Our investigation of these religions, as Dr. Read suggests, ought not to be a noting of inferior alternatives, but ought to seek to develop sympathetic appreciation and to reduce barriers of distrust and misunderstanding. Most of us see readily that this is the attitude we ought to try to take if we were living among Moslems or Buddhists. This is the attitude I try to take as a Mormon living among heretics and Gentiles and I believe it is the attitude I would try to take if I were a Gentile or a heretic living among the Mormons.

THOMAS F. O'DEA

As the chairman has more or less suggested by implication, I think I am the outsider in a certain way in this discussion tonight, and by that I mean that the hidden phonograph under my pillow did not play "I am a Mormon boy." It may have played something else to the same tune, but it did not play that.

Professor Waldemer Read, my very good friend and esteemed colleague, has given tonight an example — an embodiment would be a better word — of that utterance of Socrates, "the unexamined life is not fit for human beings." Whatever criticisms we may make of the local culture, it is to its great credit that it can produce a man like Waldemer Read. I feel naturally a certain — timidity is not the word, I have not been terribly noted for that — a certain reticence perhaps in moving into this subject because, as I say, I do speak as an outsider. I will remind you before I begin, not as a commercial, but simply as a qualification, that I also wrote another book about another religious group, one with which I have been identified, a book which was quite critical, and if I say critical things here tonight about Mormonism in commenting on these remarks of Professor Read's, I do it as a sympathetic outsider trying to understand.

The first general statement I would make would be this — that institutions that claim to speak for God shoulder a heavy responsibility, a heavy responsibility indeed, and the kinds of questions which Professor Read raises are not ones that ought to be lost because of routine, dogma, etc.

Secondly, I would like to quote a statement of the noted contemporary Protestant theologian, Paul Tillich. I paraphrase it because I quote it from memory. He said that the Old Church — you realize that when Tillich speaks of the Old Church, he is not speaking of the LDS Church, I presume — was the school mistress of Europe until the fourteenth century. But from that point on it could not handle the maturation and individuation of its pupil. I think there is a great deal of truth in this characterization of the Catholic Church by a noted Protestant theologian. I suggest that thinking Latter-day Saints may well ponder the statement and may well wonder if any analogues of it may be applicable to their own immediate situation.

I would like to point out just a couple of things that came to my mind when I heard this address of Professor Read's tonight. We live in the midst of a great technological revolution which is changing the very basic ontological status of man upon this globe. The industrial revolution is a mild name for it. It is the age of a new technology. Now, it is interesting that in the Christian tradition, both Protestantism and Catholicism have long wrestled with the problem of an ethical confrontation of this revolution and what is to be done about it. I hesitate to mention in Utah that a recent encyclical of the Pope has more or less done what many Utah politicians would call endorse the welfare state. I presume that the local Catholics in Utah probably do not agree with the Pope on this — but that is irrelevant — I am presuming that in their defense. The point is, that I do not see coming out of Mormon thinking anything comparable to the Protestant or Catholic product on this score. Nor do I see the evidence that this kind of thinking is taking place.

The second problem that came to my mind as I heard this speech, and as I read it before I heard it, is that the question of the relation between religion and liberal learning and science is a problem to which I feel once again the Mormon Church has not addressed itself in a way that faces up to all the thorny and intricate difficulties involved. The methodological answer is not sufficient in speaking of science. It is not enough to lay out a nice little positivistic methodology for science and then another set of things for value judgments, and then to say, "Well, you see they have nothing to do with each other." This is not enough of an answer because the findings of science, the attitudes of mind which have derived out of scientific experience affect the whole cast of human thinking, and it is with this whole cast of human thinking, with this whole reformation of human awareness and human consciousness with which religion has to contend and which it has to face up to in handling these questions. From Copernicus to the present time we have come from the closed world to the open universe, and the amount of adjustment, of rethinking, of critical reappraisal — of anguished reappraisal, I guess — agonized reappraisal, to use a good Republican phrase — the amount of that that has gone into this sort of thinking is tremendous. I do not see that kind of thing happening too much in Utah — maybe I am not in the right circles I will be told — but I really do not see too much of it happening. Turning to another matter:

Within Mormon theology itself (even though I am not of LDS background and not a member of the LDS Church, I have read a certain amount of Mormon theological writings, and I am fairly well acquainted with Mormon scriptural sources), I am very firmly of the opinion, which I could document were there time, that there are two strands in Mormon thinking: that strand which I would say is summed up in the Book of Mormon and which generally speaking is biblical and is a re-presentation of the biblical viewpoint; and that strand which one sees unfolding and developing in the Doctrine and Covenant and the Pearl of Great Price. I am, as an outsider — and I say this in all humility — I am rather astounded by the fact that Mormon religious thinking has not felt the necessity to come to grips with, what seem to me, the contradictions in these two strands in the way in which the early fathers of the church felt it was necessary to come to grips with certain of the implications in Christian beliefs and to try to work out a consistent, logical, rational synthesis of the two.

I raise these two problems because I think they are evidences of the things Professor Read spoke about. I think that because of these contemporary omissions many of the important values that have informed Mormonism, infused Mormon community life, made the early history of pioneering effort and accomplishment of the Mormon group so great are being sold short by a kind of unconscious routinization which seems to have, if I may be permitted the phrase, come upon you in these latter days.

LEWIS M. ROGERS

Ladies and gentlemen, we have had a most difficult task undertaken here this evening. As you know, it is not easy to bell a cat, especially a fairly large and sensitive cat. To do *this* with gentleness and restraint requires unusual skill and diplomacy. I felt that our speaker was most successful in nailing down the salient aspects of the question: What Freedom Exists in The Local Culture? The approach was forthright, the figures of speech were artistically and effectively drawn. The meaning was clear. (No one, I suppose, missed the point.) Yet it seemed to me that the "job" was done with restraint and dignity and without offense to any person or to any group.

I should like to call your attention to one or two preliminary details about which I shall briefly comment: The first relates to introductory statements that special significance had been claimed for the ringing of the Nauvoo bell. I desire here only to say that I was unaware that such *distinctive* claims for freedom had been made. On the other hand, I think I would have been somewhat surprised if, in the light of events at Nauvoo in early LDS church history, some such meanings had not become a part of the Mormon tradition. It is unfortunate that while the Nauvoo bell continues to ring and while proclamations guaranteeing freedom to worship according to the dictates of one's own conscience are frequently recited, neither of these, bell nor article of faith, seem to have caused any general deepening of insights among members as to the nature of the more serious threats to their freedoms.

Our country faces serious danger at home and abroad. We have not time to concern ourselves with any but the salient issues, peace and the preservation of our liberty. The substitution of pseudo-problems or peripheral objectives for the real ones will certainly contribute to our defeat. For many persons in our culture it has become easy to label all proposals for change as "wicked" and any person whose views differ from their own as "pink." Reasonableness and the right to free expression must prevail among our people. The preservation of our freedoms depends upon it. It is most vital, therefore, for us to commit our resources to the support of these things without fear of intimidation from either Left wing or Right wing extremists and to encourage free expression as one major resource of our strength.

My second comment concerns the words, "local culture." There can be scarcely any question in the minds of those present as to whom or as to what these terms refer. However, it should be observed that there are important elements in this culture other than the LDS Church — other churches, social groups and persons, even members of the Mormon Church itself — who, despite certain pressures and controls (and I am not prepared to say that such pressures are intentional), have insisted upon and successfully maintained their rights to be free, to be autonomous, creative and productive. While the polar elements essential for cultivation of freedom are certainly lacking within the orthodox body, as Professor Read points out, there does exist considerable creative tension between Mormon and non-Mormon elements in the culture and between the orthodox, conservative Mormon and his opposite, the Mormon liberal.

As I reflected upon the meaning and import of this paper, one question came up before my mind continually: why are self-examination and self-correction so often as difficult as they are? After all, criticism is a perfectly legitimate undertaking for mature men and women. We analyze works of art and literature; we criticize governments and other local cultures. Why, then, this willingness to suspend critical judgment when it comes to the dominant social-religious institution in our own culture? I believe that Professor Read met this issue squarely in his analysis of certain methodological beliefs characteristic of the culture; namely, belief in the absolute certainty of doctrine and belief in the final authority of hierarchy and organization.

But it occurred to me that the question of freedoms in the local culture has become further complicated by its involvement with the moods and tensions of a broader context. The threat of Russian imperialism, the spread of Communist doctrines in the resurgent areas of the world and the fear of nuclear war have resulted in a general atmosphere of anxiety. As a consequence, striving for security has become one of the most powerful forces in our society, a force which explains in part the current trend toward absolutism in LDS theology. After a delay of some twenty years, neo-orthodox-like doctrines stressing the impotence of man and the carnal and the sensual in human nature, popular themes among European theologians in the post-war period, are finally beginning to take hold in local theological discourse. Optimistic estimates of man which were somewhat more characteristic of earlier Mormon thought are gradually yielding to pessimistic themes. Absolutistic doctrines emphasizing man's complete dependence upon God, church hierarchy and organization have found reinforcement in the security needs of our era, and so long as this emphasis continues among theologians and church administrators, freedom for the individual is not likely to become a lively matter of concern.

I am in agreement with our speaker that there are those true to the faith who have made a fetish of belonging. In numerous instances the call for unity or the call to lose one's self in service to God have been interpreted as calls to serve the institution or as calls to conformity. As a consequence, much needed energy, enthusiasm for worthy causes and administrative genius have been drained away in the pursuit of peripheral objectives or dissipated in church business. It is my contention, and in this I concur with the thesis of this essay, that to urge a unity within the institution which eventuates in dependence upon it or to urge naïve obedience to external authorities, in short, to preserve the dependent child-adult, is inimical to the cause of freedom. All too frequently one hears the question, "But what do we believe?" Obviously, they mean, "What does my own church prescribe?" Apparently, a few feel the necessity to declare their own beliefs. As the British writer, Colin Wilson, pointed out, we live in an age of anti-heroes. For most persons security and adjustment to the group seem to be more highly prized than heroic risk-taking. After all, it is safe and comfortable to belong, and to lean upon external authorities requires no risk to one's security. I call your attention to a quotation from Bertrand Russell printed on the back of the Great Issues program:

All sorts of intellectual systems — Christianity, Socialism, Patriotism, etc. — are ready, like orphan asylums, to give safety in return for servitude. A free mental life cannot be as warm and comfortable and sociable as a life enveloped in a creed: only a creed can give the feeling of a cozy fireside while the winter storms are raging without.

It seems to me that the chief function of the church, any church, for that matter, is to help liberate men from all forms of crippling dependence. This means that it ought not cling to its members for the purpose of expanding or enriching its own institutional structure. On the contrary, it ought to encourage them to let go of their crutches. It ought to send men and women forth to assume roles of responsibility and to take up tasks which will promote goodwill in the world. But, somehow, I have the feeling that the church has not visualized its mission in these terms.

Sometime ago a colleague and I were commenting upon the obedience-conformity patterns in our local culture and in the course of the discussion he employed a very striking and what I thought a devastating figure of speech. Mormon liberals, he said, are like the pebbles on the shoulder of a new, hard-surfaced highway. They have been pushed there by graders. Other pebbles in the center of the road have been smashed flat into a solid and level mass by the steam roller which passes over them. What makes a liberal think he can do anything to make those pebbles rise to the surface again?

I share the pessimism, or perhaps I should say, the realism, expressed by this figure. Likewise, I share Professor Read's conviction that exclusiveness, built-in isolationism and dogmatism make the cultivation of the idea of freedom in this culture extremely difficult. However, the pessimism *I feel* extends primarily to the institution itself and to its most conservative core. I still find myself speaking and acting as though something can be done with persons whom I choose to refer to as "an unfaithful remnant."

In one of his popular essays, William James once made the observation that "social evolution is the resultant of the interaction of two wholly distinct factors — the individual . . . and the social environment." [1] But he says the individual bears "all the power of initiative and origination in his hands." "There is very little difference between one man and another," he continues, "but what little there is, *is very important*." [2] It seems to me that in our case what little difference exists among persons of our local culture is the basis of our hope.

In my estimation, this is an excellent paper. I am deadly serious when I say it ought to appear in the *Improvement Era*.

---

[1] William James, *The Will to Believe, Human Immortality and Other Essays on Popular Philosophy* (Dover Publications, 1956), p. 232.

[2] *Ibid.*, pp. 256, 257.